St. Johns River

An Illustrated History

Donald D. Spencer

Schiffer
Publishing Ltd

4880 Lower Valley Road, Atglen, Pa 19310

Other Schiffer Books by Donald D. Spencer
Greetings from Daytona Beach, 978-0-7643-2806-0, $24.95
Greetings from Ormond Beach, 978-0-7643-2809-1, $24.95
Greetings from Tampa, 978-0-7643-2898-5, $24.95
Greetings from St. Augustine, 978-0-7643-2802-2, $24.95

Other Schiffer Books on Related Subjects
Greetings from St. Petersburg, 978-0-7643-2690-5, $24.95
St. Petersburg: Past and Present, 978-0-7643-2903-6, $24.95
Miami Beach Postcards, 0-7643-2306-7, $14.95

Copyright © 2008 by Donald D. Spencer
Library of Congress Control Number: 2008924687

Designed by RoS
Type set in Souvenir Lt BT

ISBN: 978-0-7643-2826-8
Printed in China

Schiffer Books are available at special discounts for bulk purchases for sales promotions or premiums. Special editions, including personalized covers, corporate imprints, and excerpts can be created in large quantities for special needs. For more information contact the publisher:

Published by Schiffer Publishing Ltd.
4880 Lower Valley Road
Atglen, PA 19310
Phone: (610) 593-1777; Fax: (610) 593-2002
E-mail: Info@schifferbooks.com

For the largest selection of fine reference books on this and related subjects, please visit our web site at **www.schifferbooks.com**
We are always looking for people to write books on new and related subjects. If you have an idea for a book please contact us at the above address.

This book may be purchased from the publisher.
Include $3.95 for shipping.
Please try your bookstore first.
You may write for a free catalog.

In Europe, Schiffer books are distributed by
Bushwood Books
6 Marksbury Ave.
Kew Gardens
Surrey TW9 4JF England
Phone: 44 (0) 20 8392-8585; Fax: 44 (0) 20 8392-9876
E-mail: info@bushwoodbooks.co.uk
Website: www.bushwoodbooks.co.uk
Free postage in the U.K., Europe; air mail at cost.

Contents

About the Postcard

Postcards had their beginning in Austria in 1869. The United States government began to issue postcards in 1873. The cards were stamped on one side to provide for the address and left blank on the other side. The picture postcard did not come into common use in the United States until after 1900. It was about 1902 that the postcard craze hit the country, lasting up to our entry into World War I in the spring of 1917. Collectors would send postcards to total strangers in faraway places, asking for local cards in return. Some collectors specialized in railroad depots, street scenes, cemeteries, churches, courthouses, farms, amusement parks, rivers, Steamboats, plants, agricultural products, even comic cards; others collected anything they could find. Postcard albums, bought by the millions, were filled with every sort of postcard ever issued. The craze was actually worldwide, since many countries had postcards.

Before March 1, 1907, it was illegal to write any message on the same side of the card as the address. For that reason the early postcards often have handwriting all over the sides of the picture, and sometimes right across it. Many an otherwise beautiful card was defaced in this way. When postcards first started to go through the mail, they were postmarked at the receiving post office as well as that of the sender, making it easy to see the time spent between post offices—sometimes remarkably brief! The volume of postcards was an important reason for discontinuing the unnecessary second marking about 1910. For years postcards cost only a nickel for six and the postage was a penny, right up to World War II.

The most popular American postcards up to World War I were those made in Germany from photographs supplied by American publishers. At the time of the postcard craze, of course, color photography was still something of a rarity and not commercially viable. For the color cards, black and white photos were touched up, hand-colored, and then generally reproduced by lithography. Lithography consists of transferring the image to a lithographic stone, offset to a rubber blanket, and then printed onto paper. The details in the German produced cards were extremely sharp, and the best of them technically have never been matched since. The German postcard industry folded up in the summer of 1914, when the war struck Europe, and never revived. Three years later, the United States entered the war, and the postcard craze ended.

Postcards printed in America were generally of a poorer quality and had a white border. These white border cards were produced until about 1930 when the "linen" textured card was introduced. While this card was less expensive to produce, it also reduced the clarity of detail in the pictures. After 1945 the "chrome" card with a glossy finish replaced the linen card. This type of finish allowed for a very sharp reproduction of the picture. In 1970, a king-sized chrome card (4-inch by 5.875-inch) was introduced and by 1978 it was in general use everywhere.

Introduction

The St. Johns River begins in the swamps southwest of Melbourne, flowing north from its source in a marshland near Lake Helen Blazes, which is just north of Lake Okeechobee. The longest river in Florida, St. Johns travels through many lakes, communities, forests, and swamps for 310 miles to its outflow in the Atlantic Ocean near Jacksonville. A meandering and slow-flowing river, the total drop of the river from source to mouth is less than thirty feet, or about one inch per mile, making it one of the "laziest" rivers in the world. This mighty stream is fed in its upper waters by hundreds of rivers, lakes, and boiling springs. The width of the river varies. It is a broad marsh at its headwaters and averages more than two miles in width between Palatka and Jacksonville. It widens to form large lakes in Central Florida. In the 1800s and early 1900s, steamboats billowing black clouds of smoke turned the river into Florida's first highway of commerce.

Naming the River

St. Johns River is Florida's greatest river and one of the world's most beautiful. Native Americans named the river Welaka, meaning "River of Lakes." Spanish explorers who noted its existence in the 1500s called it Rio de Corrientes, "River of Currents." On May 1, 1562, French Huguenots (Protestants) rediscovered the river and called it the "River of May," to commemorate the date of their arrival and, perhaps, for its lush subtropical beauty. When the Spanish recaptured the river in 1565, they renamed it for the saint whose feast day followed the day of its capture, San Mateo. In the early seventeenth century the river came to be called by the name of the mission near its mouth, the San Juan. When the British acquired the river in 1763, they kept that name, translating it into English—"the St. Johns."

A River Scene Near Palatka.
Alligator Border postcards are a series of 165 colored, divided back, topical postcards of early Florida scenes surrounded by a border of three embossed alligators. They were very popular in the early 1900s, and today are collector items. They were published by S. Langsdorf and Company in New York and printed in Germany before World War I. This view is of the St. Johns River. Circa 1910, $30-100.

Along the River Banks.
This view shows a peaceful scene on the St. Johns River. Alligator Border postcards have a unique design and the quality of printing excellent. Many postcard collectors save these cards and prices are steadily advancing. Circa 1910, $30-100.

Live Oak on the St. Johns.
A large Live Oak sharing the bank of the St. Johns River with a variety of other trees. Circa 1910, $30-100.

Historical Sites

Many archeological and historical sites are located along St. Johns River, and several significant underwater sites have been discovered. Numerous shell mounds and middens are evidence of the Indian civilizations that developed 10,000 years ago along the river. The middens—huge shell piles—affirm the importance of the river as a food source.

The original site of Fort Caroline, a 1564 French settlement near the mouth of the St. Johns River, was washed away in the 1880s, but a replica has been erected nearby to help visitors visualize the scene. The remains of the colonial Fort Picolata is also located along the St. Johns River. The wreckage of Union supply boats, sunk as a result of Confederate mine warfare, lie on the river's bottom near Jacksonville.

Tourist Attraction

St. Johns River was one of the first tourist attractions in Florida, and hotels lined its banks from Jacksonville to Sanford. Steamboats plied the river in the period between the late 1800s and the early 1900s. Some of the first citrus groves in the state were located along the northern shores of St. Johns. Steamboat passengers coming from the north enjoyed strolling through the orange groves and picking tree-ripened fruit.

Steamboats on the River

The first steamboat to ply the waters of the St. Johns River — and the first in Florida — was the *George Washington* in 1830. In 1834 the steamer *Florida* was running more or less regularly between Savannah and Picolata on the St. Johns, and in the 1840s, the *Sarah Spaulding* plied between Jacksonville and Lake Monroe. *The Darlington* came in 1852 and was the regular boat between Jacksonville and Enterprise up to the time of the Civil War. During the Civil War, Federal gunboats swept St. Johns clear of river steamboats, but when peace was declared, a few of the old boats found their way back into the trade. *The Darlington* returned and was the pioneer boat on the river for many years.

In 1867 the Brock Line of steamboats was organized and included the *Hattie, Darlington,* and *Florence*. The DeBary Line, which originated in 1876, became the largest steamboat line on the river. In 1883, the DeBary Merchants Line and another large steamboat line, H. T. Baya Line, consolidated to become the DeBary-Baya Merchants Line. The DeBary Steamboats were the *George M. Bird, Anita, Fannie Dugan, Rosa, Welaka, Everglade, Frederick DeBary,* and *City of Jacksonville*. The Baya Line Steamboats were the *Gazelle, Water Lily, Spitfire, Georgea, Magnolia, Pastime, H. T. Baya,* and *Sylvan Glen*. In 1889 the DeBary-Baya line was absorbed by the Clyde Line and became the Clyde St. Johns River Line. Ed Mueller, in his book *St. Johns River Steamboats,* lists the complete details of over 150 vessels plying the St. Johns River from 1830 to 1910.

s 540 *The 'Crescent' on the St. John's River. Palatka, Florida.*

Left: Frederick De Bary *Steamboat.*
A trip by riverboat steamer along the wild and weird St. Johns River was one of the greatest attractions for all Florida tourists in the 1800s and early 1900s. Gliding along the river, visitors saw large orange groves, flourishing little communities, exotic sub-tropical vegetation, and interesting wildlife, including Alligators. A panorama completely different to the Northern visitors, but one remembered vividly long after the boat trip was over. This Alligator Border postcard shows the *Frederick DeBary* Steamboat. This iron-hulled, side-wheeler vessel was 145.5 feet long and 24.2 feet wide. The *Frederick DeBary* ran daily from Jacksonville to Enterprise on Lake Monroe. Among her famous passengers was President Chester Arthur. Circa 1910, $30-100.

The *Crescent* on the St. Johns River.
The eighty-four gross ton, steel-hull, 120-foot long *Crescent* Steamboat was built in 1893 in Jacksonville. This Alligator Border postcard shows the *Crescent* sailing on St. Johns River near Palatka. Circa 1910, $30-100.

7

Major Communities & Steamboat Landings

The major cities, towns, and steamboat landings on the St. Johns River were Jacksonville, Mandarin, Magnolia, Green Cove Springs, Tocoi, Palatka, Welaka, Volusia, Astor, DeLand, Blue Spring/Orange City, Sanford, and Enterprise.

The following is a list identifying the steamboat landings on the St. Johns River and their distance from Jacksonville. The DeBary-Baya Merchants Line published the (list) in the early 1880s.

Mulberry Grove, 12 miles; Mandarin, 15 miles; Hibernia, 23 miles; Magnolia, 28 miles; Green Cove Springs, 30 miles; Picolata, 44 miles; Tocoi, 49 miles; Federal Point, 58 miles; Orange Mills, 63 miles; Palatka, 75 miles; San Mateo, 79 miles; Edgewater, 80 miles; Buffalo Bluff, 87 miles; Nashua, 95 miles; Welaka, 100 miles; Beecher, 101 miles; Norwalk, 103 miles; Mount Royal, 105 miles; Fruitland, 105 miles; Fort Gates, 106 miles; Pelham Park, 112 miles; Georgetown, 113 miles; Lake George, 115 miles; Drayton Island, 116 miles; Seville, 120 miles; Spring Grove, 126 miles; Volusia, 134 miles; Astor, 134 miles; Manhattan, 136 miles; Bluffton, 140 miles; Hawkinsville, 160 miles; DeLand, 162 miles; Beresford, 163 miles; Cabbage Bluff, 165 miles; Blue Spring, 168 miles; Sanford, 193 miles; Mellonville, 195 miles; and Enterprise, 198 miles

Looking Across the River.
A scene at Palatka looking toward Hart's Point across St. Johns River. Circa 1910, $30-100.

The Upper St. Johns

Enterprise and Sanford was, for the tourist, the head of navigation on the river. However, the more adventurous could penetrate a full hundred miles farther on, slightly east and then south, toward the indefinite sources of the St. Johns. Concerning its uncharted streams, its bogs of sawgrass, its unending palmetto hammocks, and its broad treeless stretches of empty and infirm meadowlands, no assured knowledge existed. One knew only that this wilderness was the home of Alligators, Bears, Raccoons, Deer, Wild Turkeys, Snakes, all sorts of Birds, Turtles, and a few less socially incommunicative, weather-tanned Florida Crackers. Thousands of Wild Ducks flocked to St. Johns each winter, to feed on the seeds of wild sunflowers.

In distinction from the clearly outlined section of the river between Jacksonville and Enterprise, known as the Lower St. Johns, this southern part, which paralleled the east coast of Florida from Titusville to Vero Beach, was called the Upper St. Johns.

A few small towns started to develop south of Enterprise and Sanford, such as Orlando, and to the southeast, Titusville and Rockledge. These towns were served indirectly by the St. Johns from a number of small Steamboats. These Steamboats connected with larger vessels at Enterprise and Sanford; and from these cities transported their freight and passengers to landings on Lake Jessup (for Orlando), or Salt Lake (for Titusville), or Lake Poinsett (for Rockledge), or at times on Lake Washington, for places yet farther south. Oxcarts and stagecoaches would then carry the freight or passengers from the lake landings to the towns. Production of oranges in the vicinity of Lakes Jessup and Harney utilized the Steamboat service into the early 1900s.

At the Wharf.
Steamboat passengers on St. Johns River often stopped in Palatka for an overnight stay or to transfer to another Steamboat going to Silver Springs or Crescent City on Crescent Lake. Palatka was a St. Johns River city that was located midway between Jacksonville and Sanford. In the 1880s, twenty-five or thirty Steamboats could usually be counted at the wharf every day and tourists sometimes had to beg for accommodations in a town of nine hotels and five hundred rooms. Circa 1910, $30-100.

The Tributaries of St. Johns River

Major tributaries, or smaller streams, creeks and rivers that flow into the St. Johns River include the Ocklawaha River; the Wekiva River; the Econlockhatchee River; Dunn's Creek, which connects St. Johns with Crescent Lake; Ortega River; Deep Creek; Juniper Creek; Blue Spring Run; and Alexander Springs Creek.

Ocklawaha River

The Ocklawaha is one of Florida's major rivers and a tributary of St. Johns. Like the St. Johns River, it flows northward. It is one of eight major rivers in the world that flows from south to north. The Ocklawaha River is 130 miles in length and consists of many hairpin turns, tortuous bends, narrow passageways, shallow areas, and obstructions. The Ocklawaha is buffered by the Ocala National Forest, which occupies approximately forty miles of the east river corridor. This popular recreational area of 378,000 acres was established in 1908.

There are many significant archaeological and historic sites along the river. The majority are reminders of the Timucua Indians, once extant in the area; twelve Indian mounds and an equivalent number of shell mounds and middens have been identified, as have artifact scatters and prehistoric campsites.

The Ocklawaha River was home to a Seminole Indian tribe. Seminole leaders Osceola and Caocoochee and their followers caught fish from the river and nourished themselves on the abundant wildlife that roamed the riverbanks. Land designated for them in Central Florida in 1768 was a utopia for the Seminoles. To them the Ocklawaha River was merely an artery in the body of their land.

On the Ocklawaha River.
The *Astatula* Steamboat, traveling on the picturesque Ocklawaha River, is illustrated on this Alligator Border postcard. The Ocklawaha flows over sixty miles in a northerly direction to St. Johns River. Its primary tributary is the Silver River, the outflow from Silver Springs. A passenger in 1902 stated, "The visitor to Florida who misses a trip up the Ocklawaha River on one of the famous river Steamboats of the Hart Line fails to behold the greatest attraction of the state." Circa 1910, $30-100.

Ocklawaha River Boats

In the 1800s, specially designed Steamboats were built for navigation on the Ocklawaha River. These boats were propelled by a small recessed wheel built in the stern to protect it from snags, logs, and the shallow and narrow passage of the Ocklawaha River. The names of some of these boats were: *Astatula, Alligator, Ocklawaha, Marion, Okeehumkee, Forrester, Tuskawilla, Silver Spring, Osceola, Hiawatha, William Howard*, and *Metamora*.

Springs Along the River

Popular Springs along the St. Johns River included Magnolia Springs, Green Cove Springs, Salt Springs, Juniper Springs, Alexander Springs, De Leon Springs, and Blue Spring.

Silver Springs, which feeds the Silver River, Ocklawaha River, and in turn the St. Johns River, is the largest artesian spring in Florida.

In the late 1800s and early 1900s it was "the thing" for tourists to go on Steamboats from Palatka to the fancy resort at Silver Springs. Thousands of visitors each year rode the picturesque Ocklawaha River Steamboats to the springs.

Hazards and Disasters

Along with the benefits of faster and more comfortable travel by Steamboat, came the inevitable, but unforeseen accidents. Accidents on the St. Johns River fell into four main categories: fire, explosion, collision, snags, and other obstructions.

Fires were an ever-present hazard on Steamboats. All the ingredients to feed a blaze were there: a wooden boat with a flimsy flammable superstructure, covered with coat upon coat of paint, and carrying a cargo of cotton or hay and piles of wood. The boilers were at the center of the flashpoint. It only needed a hot ember to shoot out from the stokehold, or a spark from the high chimney to fall unobserved into the right place to set off an inferno.

Moored craft were subject to additional hazards in the crowded docks where boats were tied up with little or no space between them. If one boat caught fire, it could quickly ignite the other steamers. The *Frederick DeBary* burned at a Jacksonville wharf in December 1883.

The most spectacular of Steamboat disasters were caused by exploding boilers. Flying wreckage, scalding water, escaping steam, and cries from the injured added to the event. Excessive pressure, lack of water in the boilers, safety valve failures, and a general lack of scientific understanding of the problems in this new form of power, were the basic reasons for such catastrophes.

Collisions were often brought about by operator confusion or poor visibility, and caused more damage to the vessels than to passengers and crew. Any loss of life was usually a result of people falling off the boat.

Sometimes disasters occurred that were related to acts of nature. Accidents caused by snags fell into this category. Snags could cause minor damage to paddle wheels and guards, but the worst damage occurred when they penetrated the hull. Some of these dangerous snags were as large as tree trunks, and as much as seventy-five feet long, waterlogged, and extremely heavy.

There were many recorded Steamboat disasters on the St. Johns River, some of which are described as follows.

During the Civil War, the *Maple Leaf*, a Union Steamboat hit a mine in the St. Johns River and immediately sank. Four people were killed and all cargo was lost. The *Maple Leaf* was delivering equipment to Jacksonville. In December 1875 the Savannah-based *Lizzie Baker* wrecked in the St. Johns on a sandbar. In 1878 the stern-wheeler *Starlight* burned and sank on Lake Monroe without any casualties. In 1882 nine people perished as the *City of Sanford* burned near Palatka. Also in 1882 the stern-wheeler *Isis* sank in a winter storm on Lake George and three people died.

The side-wheeler *Roxie*, which made runs from Astor to and from Leesburg, burned in late 1882. The *Chesapeake* collided with the *Chattahoochee* on the St. Johns in March 1885. In July 1889 the *Queen of St. Johns* Steamboat caught fire and completely burned. The *Metamora* hit a snag in the Ocklawaha River and sank in 1903. The *Hiawatha*, often called the "Queen of the Ocklawaha River," sunk at Hart's Point in East Palatka in 1919. She slowly disintegrated there and was finally removed in 1979.

On April 29, 1890 the 137-foot, steel-hulled *H. B. Plant*, loaded with forty-one passengers, was destroyed by fire as it approached Deerfoot Landing on Lake Beresford. The burning steamer's paddle wheel stopped half a mile from the landing. The Steamboat was the key vessel in the St. Johns River fleet of railroad magnate Henry Bradley Plant. She made the fifteen-hour run three times a week from Jacksonville to Sanford, carrying mail, freight, and passengers to river settlements. The *H. B. Plant* fire was the worst Steamboat accident on the Upper St. Johns. Many accidents occurred on the Lower St. Johns River where river traffic was heavy. In 1899, a second *H. B. Plant* Steamboat was built in Jacksonville and ran routes on Florida's west coast. It burned at a Tampa pier in 1913.

Wildlife

In his travels in the 1700s, William Bartram marveled at the abundance of fish and wildlife along the river. The native peoples had been reaping the bounty of the fishery for centuries, and new settlers followed suit.

A wide variety of plant and animal species are located all along the river. Approximately 170 fish species have been reported in the St. Johns. Besides being a playground for anglers and boaters, the undeveloped banks of the St. Johns River are sanctuaries for Great Blue Herons, Egrets, Sandhill Cranes, Wood Storks, Pelicans, Eagles, Ospreys, Ibis, Bittern, and Limpkin. Alligators are plentiful in the river. Deer, Black Bear, Raccoons, Turtles, Wildcats and other wild animals are often found along the banks of the river.

The River Today

The St. Johns River provides for industry, agriculture, and recreation. Watercrafts from canoes to 85,000-ton U.S. Navy aircraft carriers know its waters. In 1998, the St. Johns River, with a rich history reaching back thousands of years to its French, Spanish and pre-historic origins, was named to the elite group of American Heritage Rivers. The waterway has won its rightful place among the great and historic rivers of this country: the Hudson, in New York, Hawaii's Hanalei River, Michigan's Detroit River, Blackstone River in Maryland, Ohio's Cuyahoga River, the Connecticut River in New England, and the Woonasquatucket in Rhode Island. Also named on this historical river list were the Mississippi, the Potomac, the Rio Grande in Texas, the Upper Susquehanna and Lackawanna Rivers in Pennsylvania, and Willamette River in Oregon.

About this Book

St. Johns River, An Illustrated History weaves together 279 color images with intriguing facts and informative text to create an immensely enjoyable journey. Learn the river's history and about the communities that border its majestic banks and tributaries.

In putting together this book a wide variety of resources were used, including books, magazine and newspaper articles, and research reports. And needless to say, personal observation played a big role when traveling up and down this river countless times.

Among the author's fond memories of St. Johns River are a 1949 fishing trip where Cottonmouth Water Moccasins lined the narrow banks of the Upper St. Johns, water hyacinths completely carpeting the river at Palatka in 1950, establishing a temporary Marine Corp post office at the Green Cove Springs Naval Station in 1953 (this while serving in the U. S. Marine Corp), and photographing Alligators, Wading Birds, and other animals during numerous trips on the river.

It is hoped the reader will enjoy this collection of old views of Florida's main inland waterway. The author invites you to come and journey back in time and discover some of the early history of this magnificent river.

Meet the St. Johns River

St. Johns River Scene. William Bartram wrote of the Florida that he visited in the 1760s and 1770s; John J. Audubon wrote of Florida as he saw it in the 1830s. These books were significant and included early descriptions of Alligators, Birds, Snakes, and other wildlife along the St. Johns River. George Barbour, who had toured Florida with General Ulysses Grant in 1870, wrote a book, *Florida for Tourists, Invalids and Settlers*. Ledyard Bill in *A Winter in Florida* described a trip on the St. Johns River from Jacksonville to Sanford. Circa 1908, $3-5.

ON THE ST. JOHNS RIVER, FLORIDA.

Chapter One

SCENE ALONG THE ST. JOHN'S RIVER, FLORIDA.

On the Beautiful St. Johns River.
In the early days the St. Johns River was the main artery of travel for all the territory between Jacksonville and Sanford. Most of the early settlers and tourists came by Steamboat—not only to Sanford but to all of South Florida as well. River traffic had so prospered by the late 1860s, that several Steamboats were making weekly round trips from Charleston and Savannah to Jacksonville, Palatka, and other St. Johns River settlements. Circa 1908, $2-4.

St. Johns River, Fla.

River View.
The St. Johns River affords innumerable attractions to sportsmen, yachtsmen, and fishermen to indulge in their favorite pastime. The shallow areas of the river are full of Fish, and sometimes Mullet leap from the river surface six feet into the air, gleaming like silver in the sunshine. Circa 1908, $4-6.

Live Oak Trees Along the River.
Some of the Live Oak trees along the St. Johns River are three hundred years old.
Live Oak wood is extremely tough and, in the 1800s, was used for ship building.
Old Ironsides was made of Live Oak and legend has it that its sides could repel
cannon shot. Circa 1910s, $2-4.

Lone Cypress.
This Cypress
tree was located
on the St. Johns
River near San-
ford. Cancelled
1909, $2-4.

A Peaceful Scene.
The beautiful moss-draped trees overhanging this famous river
truly make this a place to relax and drink in nature's beauty.
Harriet Beecher Stowe, in her 1872 book, *Palmetto Leaves*,
wrote about life on the St. Johns River. She painted Florida
as a tropical paradise, greatly promoting the interest of the
northern tourist in Florida. Circa 1940s, $1-3.

WATER OAK ON THE ST. JOHN'S RIVER, FLORIDA.

Turpentine Still on St. Johns River, Florida.

Water Oak Tree.
A seventy-foot tall Water Oak tree on the St. Johns River; the Water Oak Tree is a rapid growing tree that produces acorns. Acorns were an important food for Florida's early Indians. They made acorn meal, soup, and mush from acorns. They also roasted acorns and scraped off mold on acorns to treat sores and inflammations. Circa 1907, $4-6.

Turpentine Still.
During the 1880s, Jacksonville became the world center for naval stores, carrying products such as pine sap, turpentine, and rosin. Thousands of acres of Pine forests were tapped to supply the demand, and numerous stills were set up to process the raw Pine tar for shipment to distant points. This view shows a Turpentine Still on the St. Johns River. Cancelled 1909, $8-10.

Pine Woods.
Pine woods, like the ones shown, were used to produce pine sap, rosin, and turpentine. Circa 1920s, $1-3.

Seining grounds on the St. Johns River, Florida.

Seining Grounds.
This view shows several fishermen on the St. Johns River. Throughout history, the river has provided Indians, settlers, and fishermen with food as well as a transportation path. Cancelled 1915, $5-7.

Water Hyacinths in Florida

Water Hyacinths on the St. Johns River.
The water hyacinth is a beautiful, free-floating, freshwater plant. Its dark green leaves rise above the water's surface from its bulb-like base, while in the center of the plant towers a spike of lavender flowers, presenting an attractive appearance. This plant was brought from Venezuela in 1884 and introduced into the St. Johns River by a lady who thought the lavender flowers would embellish her fish pond; it eventually became a troublesome weed, choking the navigable channels of the river. Manatee feed on it, but it still grows. Large expenditures of labor and money on mechanical and chemical control result in only temporary relief. Circa 1930s, $1-3.

Water Hyacinths on St. Johns River, Fla.

Churning through Water Hyacinths.
This view shows the *Everglade* Steamboat churning through water hyacinths on the St. Johns River. In the early 1900s, water hyacinths covered millions of acres of the St. Johns River and its tributaries and became a menace to Steamboat navigation. The water hyacinth, a South American aquatic plant, is considered one of the world's worst weeds. Circa 1910, $6-8.

HAULING ORANGES IN A PRIMITIVE WAY, FLORIDA

Taking Oranges to Market.
In the late 1800s and early 1900s many citrus groves were planted along the St. Johns River. This view shows workers transporting boxes of oranges from the grove to a Steamboat landing. Cancelled 1912, $12-14.

MOONLIGHT ON THE ST. JOHNS RIVER, FLORIDA.

Moonlight on the St. Johns.
For over two centuries after the Spanish established themselves in Florida, the St. Johns River was practically the
only avenue of travel to the interior of the peninsula. Circa 1910, $1-3.

Palatka River Scene.
A peaceful scene of the St. Johns River near Palatka. Copyright 1905, $6-8.

Boating on St. Johns River, Florida in January.

G 15664 Riverside, St. John's River, Palatka, Fla.

Greetings. Orlando Florida
Feb-20th 1909
(Mrs) W. L. Collamore.

11243   ST. JOHN'S RIVER, SANFORD, FLA.

Fishing and Boating on the River.
Fishing and boating has always been popular on the St. Johns River. On any day fishermen line the river with hat, cane pole, bait, cold soda, and perhaps some type of chair or seat. Many fishermen favor small boats to go out to a good spot where they set with rod and reel. Circa 1903, $6-8.

Cypress Trees.
Indians carved canoes from cypress trees. At one time Florida had extensive stands of huge cypress that were lumbered out. Canals were dredged to float lumber out of the swamps. The Bald Cypress is a very deep-rooted, slow growing conifer that grows in wet places. Circa 1908, $1-3.

Cypress Knees.
Cypress Trees grow along the banks of the St. Johns River. The "knees" apparently help aerate the roots. The knees were widely used to produce novelty items. Circa 1920s, $2-4.

Spanish Moss.
This rootless epiphyte (air plant) is commonly found on Oak Trees as the seeds can take root in rough bark. Contrary to its name, Spanish Moss is not Spanish or a moss, but a very small bromeliad, a flowering plant. Spanish Moss stores water in special structures on its surface. Circa 1904, $2-4.

Sabal Palms.
The Sabal Palm played an important part in the early history of Florida, providing both food and shelter for the settler. The young buds were eaten, the trunks were cut into logs for the walls of forts and homes, and the fronds made weather resistant roof thatching. It is Florida's State Tree. Cancelled 1912, $1-3.

Panama Park.
Parks are located along the St. Johns River from Jacksonville to Sanford. Circa 1905, $4-6.

On the beautiful St. Johns River, Florida.

IN GOD WE TRUST

On the Beautiful St. Johns River, Fla.

IN GOD WE TRUST

IN GOD WE TRUST

On the beautiful St.

Trees on the St. Johns.
Cypress, Palm, Pine, and Live Oak trees share the banks of the St. Johns River in harmony, enhancing the river's subtropical balance. Pine trees grow on the higher areas, while Palm, Oak hammocks, Cypress swamps and marshes variously border the river and its tributaries. Circa 1910s, $2-4.

Scene on
The St. Johns River,
Florida.

A Lone Cypress, Florida.

River, Florida.

A GLIMPSE OF THE ST. JOHNS RIVER, FLORIDA.

Scene on The Banks of St. Johns River,
Florida.

23

Lovers' Walk.
A picturesque walkway along the St. Johns River at Green Cove Springs.
Circa 1908, $1-3.

S-9—Fishing in Tropical Wekiwa River near Sanford, Fla.

Wekiva River.
The Wekiva River, estimated to be twenty-five million years old, is a tributary of the St. Johns River. The Seminole Indians named the river Wekiva, which means "Waters of the Springs," because it rises from the boil of the Wekiwa Springs. The springs produce forty-eight million gallons of water daily. There are prehistoric Indian mounds (middens) scattered along the banks of the river. Circa 1930s, $2-4.

The Steamboat Era

An 1875 Steamboat Trip

D. Webster Dixon, a Vermont newspaperman, visited Florida in 1875 and 1876 and wrote about his journey. The following words are extracted from his many columns published in the *St. Albans Messenger*.

After we leave Jacksonville, going southward, the first landing of any importance is Orange Park. The next landing is Mandarin, which is mainly interesting as being the winter residence of Mrs. Harriet Beecher Stowe. Her house is of moderate size, and almost obscured by the foliage of the large oak and other trees. She has an orange grove of five acres, which produced 35,000 oranges last year. Near Mandarin is the wreck of the government transport, *Maple Leaf*, sunk by a torpedo during the Civil War; only the walking beam of the engine is visible above the water. Thirteen miles below Jacksonville, on the east bank of the river, is a large Indian mount, consisting of an extensive deposit of oyster shells. The next point of interest is Hibernia, which is quite a resort for invalids. There is a good hotel and a handsome myrtle grove and walks here.

The next stopping place is Magnolia, twenty-seven miles from Jacksonville, which has a hotel and several small residences. It is one of the most pleasant resorts on St. Johns River. Black Creek, located a short distance north, contains many alligators.

Green Cove Springs, on the same side, five miles south, is the most popular resort between Jacksonville and Palatka, and is a

Palms along the Banks of the St. Johns River, Florida.

Steamboats.
The steam-powered riverboat was the first American invention of world significance; the first technical accomplishment that freed man from the limitations placed upon his movements up and down rivers by the vagaries of the wind. Steamboat travel on the St. Johns River accelerated the development of interior Florida. Circa 1920s, $4-6.

charming place. It has two large hotels, fine trees, walks, etc., but its principal attraction is a mineral spring which throws 3,000 gallons per minute; the water is strongly sulfurous, with a temperature of 75°, and of course not agreeable to the taste, but is said to be nice for bathing. The basin is thirty-five feet across and twenty-five feet deep in the center. Opposite Green Cove, on the east bank, is a similar spring at a place called Remington Park. Fourteen miles further south on the same side is Picolata, the site of an ancient Spanish settlement, but of little present interest. Five miles south of this point is Tocoi Landing, where visitors are transferred by rail to St. Augustine. From this place to Palatka there are few settlements.

At Tocoi, we take cars on the St. John Railway, for St. Augustine. The distance is fourteen miles. The train consists of a car built like a streetcar, a platform car with a canvass top and open sides, and a baggage-car, the whole drawn by a locomotive of small size. Previous to last fall the cars were drawn by mules, and the trip was quite tedious.

Palatka is on the west bank of the St. Johns, and has a population of about 1,000. It has many stores and considerable trade from the back country, one newspaper, and two hotels, much too small to accommodate the great rush of the present season. There are several handsome orange groves in this vicinity. One, immediately opposite the town, is owned by Col. Hart, and consists of 700 trees, some of them forty years old. There are so many tourists coming and going every day that it gives the place a lively

SCENE ON THE BEAUTIFUL ST. JOHNS RIVER, FLORIDA.

Steamboat Approaches the Shoreline.
Historically Florida has had two waterborne transport systems: "outside" on the Atlantic Ocean and Gulf of Mexico coasts, and "inside" on the rivers. The 1880s were the boom era for riverboat travel on the St. Johns and other Florida rivers. Steamboats transported tourists and freight to and from towns along the St. Johns. Circa 1908, $8-10.

Clyde Line Steamer City of Jacksonville, on the St. Johns River, Florida.

Popularity of St. Johns River.
In the late 1800s and early 1900s, interest in Florida was high. Florida winters were advertised in newspapers, magazines and books in such glowing terms that areas accessible by Steamboat became popular as winter residences for the affluent. With a winter home in Florida, they could escape the snow, ice, and cold of their northern homes. The St. Johns River towns became the most popular winter resorts in the nation. This postcard illustrates the *City of Jacksonville* steamer bringing visitors to the towns along the St. John River. Steamboats ran on regular schedules from Jacksonville, Orange Park, Green Cove Springs, Palatka, Enterprise, and Sanford. Circa 1907, $12-14.

appearance. There are frequently from three to six steamers at the landing at one time.

Visitors to Palatka will find something of interest at Heiss' curiosity shop. He has a tank containing a large number of living alligators. He also shows tame coons, live otters, squirrels, and several species of birds. His museum of stuffed specimens is quite extensive. Here is the "Centennial Alligator," fifteen feet long, and monster rattlesnakes and moccasins.

Palatka, being the head of navigation for large seagoing Steamboats, promises to become in time a flourishing and populous place, though it may never be a formidable rival to Jacksonville.

As we leave Palatka the St. Johns suddenly becomes narrower, and so continues until it expands into Lake George, above Welaka. Before reaching Welaka we were favored with some picturesque views of river scenery. The only places of any importance on the St. Johns above Palatka are Welaka, Volusia, Blue Spring, Enterprise, Mellonville, and Sanford.

Enterprise is the head of regular Steamboat navigation on the St. Johns. It has a large hotel and a few boarding houses, and the table fare does not receive flattering notices from visitors. Fishing and hunting expeditions are fitted out here for the upper lakes and the Indian River country. From this point, also, small steamers make excursions to the lower lakes. New Smyrna, on the Indian River, is the place where a colony of Minorcans was settled in 1767, and cultivated indigo and sugar cane. Mellonville, on Lake Monroe, 125 miles from Palatka, has handsome orange groves; also an abundance of game and fish. On Lake Monroe is a place called Sanford, which is proposed to build up for a popular resort.

Steamboat Plying the St. Johns River.
A trip by riverboat steamer along the wild and weird St. Johns River was one of the greatest attractions for all Florida tourists. Gliding along the river, visitors saw on the banks large orange groves, flourishing little communities, exotic sub-tropical vegetation, and interesting wildlife. A panorama completely different to Northern visitors, but one remembered vividly long after the boat trip was over. This view shows the *Frederick DeBary* —an iron-hulled side-wheeler vessel at 145.5 feet long and 24.2 feet wide. The *Frederick DeBary* ran daily from Jacksonville to Enterprise on Lake Monroe. Among her famous passengers was President Chester Arthur. Circa 1910, $8-10.

Picturesque Scenery.
Steamboat travel on the St. Johns River between Sanford and Palatka was very picturesque. The river in this area is narrow, tortuous, and strange, and at night, illuminated by the powerful searchlight of the Steamboats, made a sort of nocturnal fairyland to the traveler's eyes. Circa 1910, $7-9.

BOATING THROUGH TROPICAL SCENERY ON THE ST. JOHNS RIVER, FLA.

Boating through Tropical Florida.
A winter visit to the St. Johns River valley became both fashionable and a tonic prescribed by Northern doctors for their pale clients' ailments. From these humble beginnings, tourism eventually became Florida's premier industry. Circa 1915, $3-5.

DeBary Merchants Line.
In 1876, DeBary established the DeBary Merchants Line, a Steamboat line to transport items up and down the St. Johns River. By 1880 the company had four steamboats, among them the *Frederick DeBary*. In 1883 the DeBary Line merged with the Baya Line and became the DeBary-Baya Merchants Line, which operated the above boat plus twelve others: *George M. Bird, Everglade, Rosa, Welaka, Sylvan Glen, Fannie Dugan, Pastime, Magnolia, Water Lily, H.T. Baya, Florence,* and *City of Jacksonville*. The business was taken over by the Clyde St. Johns River Line in 1889. Cancelled 1911, $18-20.

On the ST. JOHNS RIVER, Florida.

3114.

FRED DEBARY

City of Jacksonville.
A view of the *City of Jacksonville* on the St. Johns River. The finest boat of the DeBary Merchants Line was 160.5 feet long, 32.5 feet wide, had a gross tonnage of 459, and a reputation of being the most successful boat ever in service on the St. Johns. Cancelled 1909, $18-20.

BEAUTIFUL ST. JOHNS RIVER, FLORIDA.

CLYDE LINE ST. JOHNS RIVER STEAMER.
"THE CITY OF JACKSONVILLE," BY NIGHT, JACKSONVILLE, FLA.

Night View of the *City of Jacksonville*.
In 1876, Frederick DeBary entered the booming Steamboat business. In 1882, he ordered, built, and finished with Florida mahogany and yellow (longleaf) pine, the *City of Jacksonville*, which became known almost immediately as the finest steamboat on the St. Johns River. Circa 1915, $6-8.

ON THE ST. JOHNS RIVER BY MOONLIGHT, FLORIDA.

Stopping for Fresh Food.
Steamboats traveling the St. Johns River would often stop to pick up fuel (wood) or food. Farms in the areas adjacent to the river brought their produce and other food items to local Steamboat landings. Circa 1915, $6-8.

Clyde Steamer Osceola, Sanford, Fla.

Osceola Approaching Sanford.
The 188-foot long *Osceola* was built in 1913. It had accommodations for 140 first-class and 100 third-class passengers. It was the last and most glorious of the St. Johns River Steamboats. People from all over the world took the leisurely trip up the river to Sanford and enjoyed listening to the colorful Captain Thomas W. Lund relate his famous stories about Alligators, including his pet with the pink ribbon around it. Circa 1913, $12-14.

Clyde Line Str. Osceola.

Osceola Steamboat.
The 474 gross ton, steel
hulled *Osceola* is shown
leaving Jacksonville. Circa
1920s, $10-12.

Upper St. Johns.
A hand-painted scene of
a small Steamboat on the
Upper St. Johns River. Circa
1910, $8-10.

Chapter Three

Small Communities Touched by the River

Souvenir Folder of the
BEAUTIFUL ST. JOHNS RIVER
Florida.

M

Communities on the St. Johns River.
In the heyday of steam boating, little settlements along the St. Johns River seemed to grow around every Steamboat landing, and spas around every sulfur spring. Wealthy Northerners created vast estates comprised of farms, citrus groves, timber operations, hunting preserves, and winter homes. In the 1880s some of the hamlets on or near the St. Johns River were Sanford, Enterprise, Blue Spring, Orange City, DeLand, Astor, Volusia, Welaka, San Mateo, Palatka, Tocoi, Green Cove Springs, Magnolia Springs, Mandarin, Orange Park, Jacksonville, and Mayport. Circa 1920s, $18-20.

Astor Landing on the St. Johns River Florida.

Astor.
A riverside settlement that remains as a relic of the once busy settlements along the St. Johns River in the 1800s. Circa 1914, $10-12.

898 Blue Spring near Orange City, Fla.

Blue Spring Run.
Blue Spring and Blue Spring Run is much more than a scenic area for swimming and canoeing. It is a place that plays a vital role in the survival of one of Florida's most precious and unique residents—the Manatee. Circa 1908, $6-8.

IN FLORIDA. Blue Springs.

Blue Spring.
A large sulfur spring of clear blue water that flows via a short stream into the St. Johns River. The water from the spring, located just west of Orange City, pours out of the ground at the rate of about sixty-five thousand gallons a minute. A group of Manatees annually migrate to the waters of this beautiful spring. This view is of tourists enjoying the spring. Circa 1908, $8-10.

Dora Canal

Chain of Lakes Cities.
Communities on the Chain of Lakes (Eustis, Leesburg, Mount Dora, and Tavares) may be reached from the St. Johns River by traveling up the Ocklawaha River to the Chain of Lakes (Lake Dora, Lake Eustis, Lake Apopka, Lake Griffin, and Lake Harris), which are interconnecting waterways. The picturesque Dora Canal connects Lake Dora and Lake Eustis. Circa 1940s, $1-3.

Crescent City, Fla.   Crescent Lake from Grove Hall.

Crescent City.
The settlement of Crescent City began to prosper in the late 1800s with the arrival of wealthy winter residents aboard Steamboats plying the St. Johns River. The settlement, located on Crescent Lake, was reached via the Dunns Creek waterway that connected Crescent Lake with the St. Johns River. Cancelled 1909, $6-8.

Crescent Steamboat.
The 84-gross ton, steel-hull, 120 foot long *Crescent* was built in 1893 in Jacksonville and is shown sailing on Crescent Lake. Circa 1910s, $10-12.

Steamer "Crescent" of Crescent City, Florida.

Crescent City, Fla., Cypress Ave.

Crescent City Street Scene.
A horse and buggy traveling on Cypress Avenue in Crescent City. Cancelled 1908, $8-10.

Greetings from DeBary.
DeBary, located on the northeast shore of Lake Monroe, is named for one of its earliest residents, Samuel Frederick DeBary. In 1870, when Debary arrived in the area, orange groves and sugar cane fields covered much of the area. He instantly fell in love with the entire area and bought four hundred acres to start a hunting and fishing preserve. DeBary Hall was built for the family's winter home. His holdings grew to 9,000 acres. Circa 1930s, $3-5.

DeBary Hall.
DeBary Hall, a southern style two-story mansion, was built in 1871 by Samuel Frederick DeBary, a Belgian wine merchant. The mansion, located on a high plateau overlooking Lake Monroe, is surrounded by great Live Oak and Pine trees. Today it is a state historic treasure; but in another time, it stood like an elegant oasis, secluded in the wild natural beauty of the St. Johns River country—a champagne watering hole where Presidents, royalty, the wealthy, and the celebrated gathered to frolic and revel, dine at gourmet banquets, or hunt and fish in a sportsman's para-

Scene on Dead River, near Eustis, Fla.

Dead River.
The Dead River, near Eustis, is about one mile in length and connects Lake Harris with Lake Eustis, in the famous Chain of Lakes, the headwaters of the Ocklawaha River, which is a major tributary of the St. Johns River. The river was named for the lack of current. The flow moves in either direction during heavy rains, as does the Dora Canal. Otherwise the river has no movement. Cancelled 1909, $3-5.

CLYDE-ST. JOHNS RIVER LINE "STEAMER OSCEOLA", AT SANFORD, FLA.

Enterprise Church.
The All Saints Episcopal Church, built in 1883, is one of the oldest original Episcopal missions in Central Florida. The white wooden, Florida Gothic (also called Carpenter's Gothic) designed church, nestled under the Live Oak trees at Enterprise, is one of the oldest sights on Lake Monroe's north shore. Circa 1940s, $5-7.

Enterprise.
The un-incorporated area in southwest Volusia County is one of the county's most historic settlements. Enterprise, founded in 1841 before Florida even became a state, served as the Volusia County seat from 1845 to 1888. Florida dissolved Enterprise's incorporation charter in 1895. Enterprise, once called Benson Springs, was once the southern terminus of St. Johns River shipping. After the Civil War, Jacob Brock built a 100-room hotel (Brock House) on Lake Monroe that attracted such dignitaries as Presidents Ulysses S. Grant and Grover Cleveland who tried their skill with rod and gun. Good food, good hunting and the excitement of the exotic wilds of Florida made the hotel popular and Captain Brock's steamboats made it accessible. *Osceola*, the largest Steamboat to travel on the St. Johns River, made regular stops at the Brock House dock as well as at the Blue Spring Landing. Cancelled 1926, $12-14.

Enterprise Spring.
This small town was once the terminus of Steamboats on the St. Johns River. Located on Lake Monroe, Enterprise was founded by Major Cornelius Taylor, and until 1888, it was the seat of Volusia County. Shown above is Green Spring, one of the attractions at Enterprise's Brock House, a popular St. Johns River resort. Circa 1907, $7-9.

GREEN SPRING. ONE OF THE ATTRACTIONS OF THE INN.   ENTERPRISE, FLA.

928 Eustis, Fla.
Gobbler's Point, Lake Eustis.

Eustis.
The community of Eustis is located on the northeast side of Lake Eustis, one of the Chain of Lakes. It is reached from the St. Johns River via the Ocklawaha River tributary. Cancelled 1908, $5-7.

Fort Florida, St. Johns River, Fla.

Fort Florida.
In 1836, during the Second Seminole War, a fort was built on the St. Johns River just north of Lake Monroe. More of a depot than a fort, it was designed to assist the garrison at Fort Mellon, the site now within the environs of Sanford, in protecting white settlements along the river against attack by angry Seminole Indians. Circa 1910s, $15-17.

Spring and Bathing Pavilion,
Green Cove Springs, Fla.

Qui-Si-Sana Hotel, Green Cove Springs, Fla.

SWIMMING POOL, GREEN COVE SPRINGS, FLA.

Green Cove Springs.
This was a fashionable spa area over a hundred years ago, attracting international patronage because of the big Qui-Si-Sana Spring, which had a flow of 3,000 gallons of sulfur water per minute. Visitors to the spa used to come in by Steamboat from Jacksonville. This Clay County city is located on the west bank of St. Johns River and was established in 1830. These views show the Qui-Si-Sana Hotel and Spa, built in 1907, one of the oldest buildings in Green Cove Springs. Circa 1910s, $4-6.

41

A. C. L. R. R. Depot, Green Cove Springs, Fla.

Green Cove Springs Depot. The Atlantic Coast Line Railroad passenger station at Green Cove Springs. Circa 1920s, $12-14.

Green Cove Springs Train Arrival. Passenger train arriving at the ACL Depot in Green Cove Springs. Circa 1920s, $12-14.

A. C. L. STATION, GREEN COVE SPRINGS, FLA.

GC.1—Small Section, "Mothball" Fleet,
U. S. Naval Station
Green Cove Springs, Fla.

Green Cove Springs Mothball Fleet.
This view shows a small section of the Navy's Reserve Fleet, moored at the Green Cove Springs Naval Station. The ships were put in a state of preservation just after World War II, to await their country's call to duty. The facility closed in 1962 and was sold to the Reynolds Aluminum Corporation. Circa 1943, $2-4.

Sports of all sorts. Howey-in-the-Hills, Florida

Howey-In-The-Hills.
Founded on Lake Harris by W. J. Howey in 1916, this citrus growing community is reached from the St. Johns River by traveling up the Ocklawaha River to the Chain of Lakes. Circa 1920s, $6-8.

Juniper Creek.
More than eight million gallons of water are produced daily at Juniper Springs. This water is channeled into the mouth of Juniper Creek, which eventually flows into Lake George and the St. Johns River. Circa 1940s, $1-3.

The Pier and St. John's River, Magnolia Springs, Fla.

Magnolia Springs.
This view shows the Steamboat dock at Magnolia Springs, twenty-seven miles south of Jacksonville. The community had a fine resort hotel and several residences. The hotel, rebuilt several times, was destroyed by fire in 1920. It was popular among tourists during the 1880s and 1890s, and included President Grover Cleveland among its guests. The President, it is said, had the spring water sent regularly to the White House. Circa 1901, $6-8.

Kingsley Plantation.
The Kingsley Plantation sits near the mouth of the St. Johns River on Fort George Island, near present day Jacksonville. The plantation was first developed in the late 1700s. Many plantations were located along the St. Johns River during the late eighteenth and early nineteenth centuries. The plantation owners shipped their products (cotton, rice, sugar, lumber, naval stores, and citrus) to northern markets using this waterway. This is an 1870s view of the Kingsley Plantation Slave Quarters. The two-room, tabby structures with brick fireplaces were still inhabited by Black slave families when this photograph was taken. Circa 1907, $10-12.

Mandarin Home of Harriet Beecher Stowe.
New England born Harriet Beecher Stowe, at age 57 in 1868, some sixteen years after her novel *Uncle Tom's Cabin* swept the nation, bought an orange grove in Mandarin, a community a few miles south of Jacksonville on the St. Johns River. Her fans up North eagerly sought out the boxes marked "Oranges from Harriet Beecher Stowe." While at Mandarin, Stowe also wrote the book *Palmetto Leaves*, about her Florida experience, which was published in 1872. Circa 1907, $4-6.

Old Home of Harriett Beecher Stowe, Author of Uncle Tom's Cabin, Mandarin, near Jacksonville, Fla.

Mandarin Sightseers.
Harriet Beecher Stowe made her winter home in Mandarin from 1868 to 1884. Northern sightseers, attracted by Mrs. Stowe's fame, would sometimes land at the wharf on the St. Johns River, roam over the place, and pick flowers and oranges. Mandarin was about a dozen miles north of Green Cove Springs. Near Mandarin is the wreck of the Union steamer, *Maple Leaf*, sunk by a mine during the Civil War. Circa 1915, $1-3.

Mayport Jetties.
The St. Johns River entrance is a major large ship channel, protected by stone jetties for nearly a mile from shore, with the channel marked by buoys for more than another mile to sea. This view shows people fishing and sunbathing on one of the jetties. Circa 1920s, $1-3.

Mount Dora.
The community of Mount Dora is located on the eastern shore of Lake Dora, one of the Chain of Lakes. It is reached from the St. Johns River via the Ocklawaha River tributary. Circa 1907, $5-7.

Orange City Hotel.
H. H. DeYarman of Wisconsin, who came to Orange City in the 1870s, built the DeYarman House in 1876 on Volusia Avenue. It served as a hotel for about seventy-five years, and was later known as the Orange City Hotel. In its heyday, the hotel included President Grover Cleveland among its guests. Circa 1907, $28-30.

Orange City Library.
The Dickinson Memorial Library was dedicated December 17, 1919. An article in the DeLand newspaper at the time described the library as without a doubt the most complete and expensive community building in the State of Florida. It was presented to the town of Orange City by Albert Dickinson of Chicago. Circa 1920s, $3-5.

Orange City Picnic.
These ladies are enjoying a picnic at the Blue Spring boil. Cancelled 1908, $6-8.

C 25—School House, Orange City, Fla.

Orange City School.
Orange City was founded in 1874 by Dr. Seth French and a group of people from Eau Claire, Wisconsin. Within a few years, the area, which was originally known as the Wisconsin Settlement, had a hotel, school, church, library, and several store buildings. In 1882 Orange City was officially organized as a town. Today, the nickname of this growing city is "Home of the Manatees," where every winter, tourists and locals flock to nearby Blue Spring to watch these gentle mammals take shelter in Blue Spring Run from the cool water of the St. Johns River. Pictured is the School House. Circa 1903, $8-9.

Blue Spring, Orange City, Fla.

Orange City Sightseeing.
The primary tourist attraction in Orange City is Blue Spring.
Circa 1908. $7-9.

BLUE SPRINGS, FLA.

Orange City Spring.
A view of Blue Spring near Orange City. Manatees (Sea Cows) can be seen here when they come to escape the cooler waters of the St. Johns River. Circa 1902, $5-7.

Graves Ave., looking East, Orange City, Fla.

Orange City Street Scene.
Southeast corner of Holly and Graves Avenue, Orange City's main street. The brick building on the right housed the Southern Express Company and is the present site of the U.S. Post Office. Circa 1907, $16-18.

Orange City-Volusia Avenue.
Throughout the 1920s, 1930s, and 1940s, businesses developed along Volusia Avenue. On the south were the DeYarman House, shown, and the Orange City Bank, which opened in 1927; to the North, Shaffer's Corner and a series of stores and other businesses stretching up the street. Circa 1908, $3-5.

Volusia Ave., looking South Orange City, Fla.

Steamer Dock on St. Johns River showing Sparhawk Hotel Orange Park Fla.

Orange Park Hotel.
Orange Park, located on the west bank of the St. Johns River just south of Jacksonville, was founded in 1876. It was named for the orange groves that flourished here during that period. Pictured are the Steamboat Dock and Sparhawk Hotel. Cancelled 1911, $5-7.

Pavilion and Steamer landing on St. Johns River Orange Park Fla.

Orange Park Steamboat Dock.
This view shows the Orange Park Steamboat Dock and Pavilion. In 1868, Harriet Beecher Stowe invested in a plantation in Orange Park for her son, Frederick, which was not a success. That same year, she purchased thirty acres at Mandarin, across the river. Circa 1907, $5-7.

A Sugar Cane Mill.

Sugar Cane Mills.
In 1763 the British were anxious to establish settlements in their new colonies. They devised a system of land grants to encourage people to locate in Florida. By the mid-1770s, there were many plantations located on the St. Johns River (including Bartram, DeBary, Hibernia, Hope Hill, Laurel Grove, Mandarin, Mount Royal, New Switzerland, Racimo, Rolle's, Spring Garden, and Tonyn). Many of these plantations raised Sugar Cane and produced granulated (crystallized) sugar from the cane. Circa 1902, $4-6.

San Mateo.
A center of orange production in the late 1800s, San Mateo was also an interesting settlement and Steamboat stop on the St. Johns River. A large orange packing house was located here. Cancelled 1916, $4-6.

A Busy Day in an Orange Grove, Florida.

Volusia Landing.
In the 1800s and early 1900s, the community of Volusia was a busy St. Johns River port. Steamboats traveling between Jacksonville and Enterprise would stop at Volusia Landing. Barrels of fish, crates of oranges, bales of cotton, animal pelts, and kegs of syrup comprised the greater part of exports; new people and food not grown locally were imports. Vessels steamed in and out of Volusia daily. This view shows a steamboat approaching Volusia Landing. Circa 1920s, $4-6.

Volusia Toll Bridge.
A covered bridge house on the St. Johns River connects Astor (in Lake County) with Volusia (in Volusia County). This toll bridge was later replaced with a newer bridge. The covered bridge house was relocated to the Pioneer Settlement for the Creative Arts, a historical museum, in Barberville. Circa 1940s, $3-5.

Welaka.
Opposite the picturesque town of Welaka, the Ocklawaha River empties into the larger St. Johns River, shown here at its grandest beauty. This early postcard view shows several moss covered Oak trees in Welaka Park along St. Johns. In 1859 there were about one hundred people living in Welaka. Circa 1907, $7-9.

The Colonial Inn   Welaka, Florida   View from the St. John's River

Welaka Hotel.
A hand-colored view
of the Colonial Inn on
the St. Johns River at
Welaka. Circa 1907,
$5-7.

Welaka, Fla. Welaka Park.

Welaka Park.
This was one of the
finest Spanish Moss-
covered Oak groves
in all of Florida. Circa
1907, $6-8.

Jacksonville

Chapter Four

On the Waterfront.

Jacksonville, which lies along the curve of the St. Johns River, has the finest natural harbor on the Southeastern Atlantic Coast, and in the late 1800s and early 1900s was the gateway to Florida by sea and land. Steamboat traffic on the St. Johns River began in 1830 when the Steamboat *George Washington* reached Jacksonville from Savannah after a run of thirty-four hours. In 1834 the Steamboat *Florida* ran regularly between Savannah and Palatka on the St. Johns. The *Essayon* carried troops and supplies up and down the river during the Seminole War. The *Darlington* came in 1852 and, up to the time of the Civil War, was the regular boat between Jacksonville and Enterprise. Except for an interval during the Civil War when U. S. gunboats stopped commercial traffic, steamboats steadily increased in number, size, and importance to the economic life of the city. In the 1880s the famous Clyde Line passenger service began. This view shows the *City of Jacksonville* Steamboat arriving at a Jacksonville dock. Circa 1910s, $12-14.

Jacksonville.
This beautiful Duval County city—the Indian name was "Wacca Pilatka," meaning "Cow Ford"—is on the north bank of the St. Johns River. Its present name was given in honor of General Andrew Jackson, the first governor of Florida. Jacksonville, incorporated in 1832, developed as a market for cotton and naval stores, and with the introduction of the steam sawmill, lumber became an important industry. By 1900, there were fewer than a million people in Florida. Jacksonville was the largest city with 28,249 people. Circa 1930s, $3-5.

City of Jacksonville Steamboat.
The Steamboat *City of Jacksonville* was part of a large river fleet that served the communities on St. Johns River. When the Clyde Line absorbed the DeBary interests in 1889, this Steamboat continued river passenger and mail service. Circa 1915, $6-8.

Florida East Coast Railway Bridge.
In 1890, railroad magnate Henry M. Flagler spanned the St. Johns River with his $1 million railroad swing bridge, which opened Florida's East Coast to train travel. This view, showing the bridge opening to allow a ship to pass, was taken from Riverside. Cancelled 1917, $3-5.

8374 ALONG THE WATER FRONT JACKSONVILLE FLA   COPYRIGHT 1904 BY DETROIT

Along the Waterfront.
In this view, a Clyde Line steamship took on passengers bound for Charleston and New York at the foot of Hogan Street. Two schooners were berthed dockside and a tug nudged a barge loaded with lumber toward its slip. Cancelled 1906, $5-7.

CLYDE-MALLORY LINER APPROACHING JACKSONVILLE, FLA.

Clyde Line Wharf and Steamer.
The Port of Jacksonville was the only port on the Atlantic Coast of Florida having both adequate rail connections and water depth to permit a full-sized ocean steamer to enter with a full cargo. Cancelled 1908, $5-7.

Northern Steamships.
At Jacksonville the St. Johns River makes a sharp turn eastward. At the mouth of the river, large steamships from New York, Charleston, and Savannah entered the river from the Atlantic Ocean. This view shows the Clyde Mallory liner *Shawnee* approaching Jacksonville on the St. Johns River. Circa 1920s, $3-5.

55

Clyde Line Steamer "Lenape," Jacksonville, Fla.

"Lenape" Steamship.
The Clyde Line steamship *Lenape* enters the Port of Jacksonville.
Circa 1910s, 5-7.

VIEW OF DOCKS AND WATER FRONT, JACKSONVILLE, FLA.

Waterfront View.
A view of the docks and waterfront at Jacksonville.
Circa 1920s, $3-5.

Aerial View of Jacksonville's Business District.

In the early 1900s Jacksonville was the principal industrial city of Florida and its influence as a leading manufacturer and distribution point extended throughout the southeast. Its landlocked port provided excellent facilities for coastwide, intercoastal, and foreign trade. Circa 1920s, $2-4.

Bird's-eye View of the Business Section, Jacksonville, Fla.

Duval Hotel. Post Office. Castle Hall. National Bank of Jacksonville. JACKSONVILLE, Fla.   3213

Jacksonville Structures.

Forsyth Street, shown from Laura Street in the years immediately following the Great Fire of 1901. The buildings in the background, at left, are the Duval Hotel, the Government Building and Post Office with its ornate tower, the Knights of Pythias' Castle Hall, and the pillared 1898 National Bank of Jacksonville, predecessor of Barnett National Bank. Barnett Banks eventually became part of the Bank of America. Cancelled 1907, $3-5.

SKYSCRAPER DISTRICT FROM THE WINDSOR, JACKSONVILLE, FLA.

Skyscraper District from the Windsor Hotel.

This view shows some of the skyscraper buildings in downtown Jacksonville. The Government Building and Post Office, and the Seminole Hotel can be seen at right. Circa 1920s, $3-5.

Hemming Park.
Hemming Park is a block-square area containing Palm, Live Oak, and Camphor trees, and landscaped with shrubs and flowers. The curved walks, lined with benches, converge at a central plaza from which rises a tall Confederate Monument, surmounted by the figure of a soldier. Today, Hemming Park is called Hemming Plaza and is as beautiful as it was in this postcard view. Circa 1920s, $3-5.

Moon over Hemming Park.
A moonlight view of Jacksonville's Hemming Park. Circa 1930s, $2-4.

Hemming Park from the Windsor Hotel.
The St. James Building as it appeared to the left of Hemming Park. Hemming Park is bordered by Duval, Hogan, Laura, and Monroe Streets. Cancelled 1925, $2-4.

Confederate Monument.
The Confederate Monument, located in the center of Hemming Park, was unveiled June 16, 1898. The park was named as a memorial to Civil War Confederate veteran Charles C. Hemming, who had donated the monument to the city in 1898. Copyright 1905, $1-3.

Main Street Bridge.
With St. Johns River flowing through its heart, and an active waterfront area, Jacksonville lives up to its nickname, "River City." Today the Main Street Bridge is called the John T. Alsop, Jr. Bridge. Circa 1930s, $1-3.

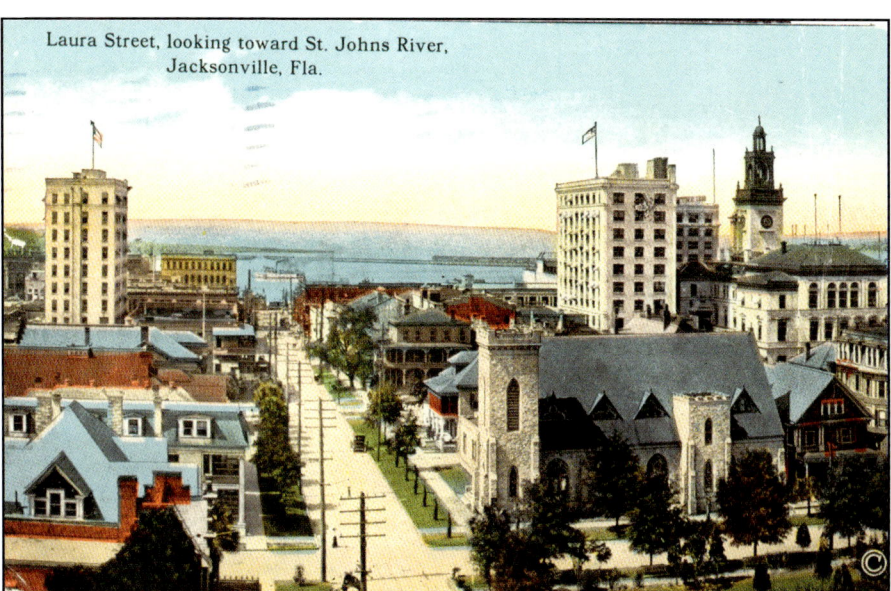

Bay Street.
In the 1890s the city's older commercial structures, west of the bridge, where the street approaches the railroad terminals, was a succession of bars, pawnshops, and upstairs hotels. By 1912, the Cohens, Furchgotts, and Levy department stores were all located on Bay Street, a street that paralleled St. Johns River in downtown Jacksonville. This view shows pedestrians in period clothing, and transportation vehicles: horse and buggy, trolley cars, and automobiles. Circa 1907, $3-5.

Laura Street.
A view of Laura Street, looking toward the St. Johns River. Cancelled 1912, $1-3.

A Busy Bay Street.
Bay Street, running parallel with and next to St. Johns River, was the main business street of Jacksonville in the late 1800s and early 1900s. Visitors were often seen trooping everywhere along the sidewalks—to the Post Office, the fruit stores, the palmetto-braiders, the curiosity shops, the wharf for a sailboat, or to a Steamboat for a trip up the St. Johns. Circa 1910s, $3-5.

Forsythe Street, Jacksonville, Fla.

Forsyth Street.
During the score of years after the 1901 fire, Jacksonville's first skyscrapers, ten stories or more, were built in the city's center. During the years to 1914 almost a dozen tall buildings were erected. This view of Forsyth Street is looking east from Hogan Street. Part of the Government Building and Post Office, and the Atlantic National Bank building are shown in the foreground. The ten-story Atlantic National Bank building was erected in 1910. Circa 1910s, $1-3.

City Hall.
The Ecole des Beaux-Arts in Paris was the most influential school of architecture, painting, and sculpture in the nineteenth century. Many prominent American architects studied there in the late 1800s and returned to design monumental public buildings in this country based on the aesthetic principle of the Ecole. Beaux-Arts buildings feature grandiose facades, adorned with towering columns, large arches, grand staircases, heavy stone bases, and ornate classical embellishments such as sculpture and bas-relief. Jacksonville's City Hall was an excellent example of this architectural style. Circa 1920s, $3-5.

Carnegie Library.
The Jacksonville Public Library, located on the northeast corner of Adams and Ocean Streets, was built in 1905. The limestone structure with a Corinthian facade was, in the early 1900s, the largest library in the state. This building, a gift from Andrew Carnegie, served as Jacksonville's main library until 1965. In 1983, it was sold for use as a private law firm. Circa 1910s, $2-4.

Carnegie Library, Jacksonville, Fla.

Jacksonville, Fla. The Court House

Duval County Courthouse.
The old Duval County Courthouse, built in 1886, had walls so stout they withstood the fire of 1901. The courthouse shown here opened in 1902. It was located on Market Street between Adams and Forsyth Streets. Circa 1910, $3-5.

PALACE THEATER, JACKSONVILLE, FLORIDA.

Palace Theater.
Although Jacksonville's first movie had been shown in 1896, the first motion theater was not opened until 1906. Movies became "talkies" in late 1927 and Jacksonville's theaters were among the first in the nation to convert. Pictured is the Palace Theater. Circa 1920s, $5-7.

Government Building and Post Office, Jacksonville, Fla.

Government Building and Post Office.
The 168-foot tower of the Government Building, northeast corner of Forsyth and Hogan Streets, stood higher than any lighthouse in the state when it was completed in 1895. The imposing Government Building housed not only the Post Office, but Government offices as well. The building survived the Jacksonville 1901 fire, but was razed in 1939-40 for the expansion of the Atlantic National Bank and for Furchgotts Department Store. Cancelled 1910, $5-7.

St. James Building and Hemming Park.
When it was completed October 21, 1912, the St. James Building was the magnum opus of Jacksonville architecture and of architect Henry John Klutho. Prior to the 1901 Fire, this site was occupied by the St. James Hotel, one of Jacksonville's grandest hotels during the 1870s and 1880s. Circa 1910s, $2-4.

Cohen Brothers Store.
Cohen Brothers, the "Big Store," was the largest department store in the State of Florida. It occupied most of the four-story St. James Building that covered an entire block. The building later became home to the May-Cohen Department Store, and in 1997 it became Jacksonville's City Hall. Circa 1930s, $1-3.

Windsor Hotel.
The Windsor Hotel was a first rank tourist hotel. It was built in 1875 on Hogan Street between Monroe and Duval Streets, facing Hemming Park. The hotel was destroyed in the 1901 fire. A "new" Windsor Hotel opened in 1902. The Windsor was of Spanish Renaissance architecture, constructed of brick, steel, and stone, and could accommodate five hundred guests. The hotel closed its doors May 1, 1950 to make way for the J. C. Penney and F. W. Woolworth department stores. Today, the Duval County Courthouse occupies the site of the former Windsor Hotel. Circa 1908, $3-5.

Jacksonville Terminal.
The stately Jacksonville Terminal, built in 1919, hosted the Seaboard Air Lines, Atlantic Coast Line, and Florida East Coast Railways. The towering Palm trees in the station plaza gave notice to travelers that they had at last reached the land of sun and surf. This building now serves as a convention center. Cancelled 1926, $5-7.

Union Railway Depot.
This view shows Jacksonville's mission-style Union Depot that was built in 1904. In 1919, this depot was replaced by the Jacksonville Terminal. The Union Depot, later used as a warehouse, was destroyed in a 1979 fire. Circa 1910s, $10-12.

Everett Hotel, Jacksonville, Fla.

Everett Hotel.
In 1873 the 150-room Grand National Hotel was built on the site of the Old Judson House, on Bay Street at Julia. The hotel was badly financed and closed in 1879. In 1881 Nathaniel Webster restored the hotel and renamed it the Everett. Over the years the Everett became the Milner and Earle Hotels and was razed in 1959. Cancelled 1912, $4-6.

HOTEL ALBERT, JACKSONVILLE, FLA.

Albert Hotel.
Automobiles wait on passengers in front of the Albert Hotel on West Adams Street. Circa 1920s, $5-7.

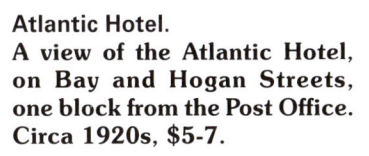

Atlantic Hotel.
A view of the Atlantic Hotel, on Bay and Hogan Streets, one block from the Post Office. Circa 1920s, $5-7.

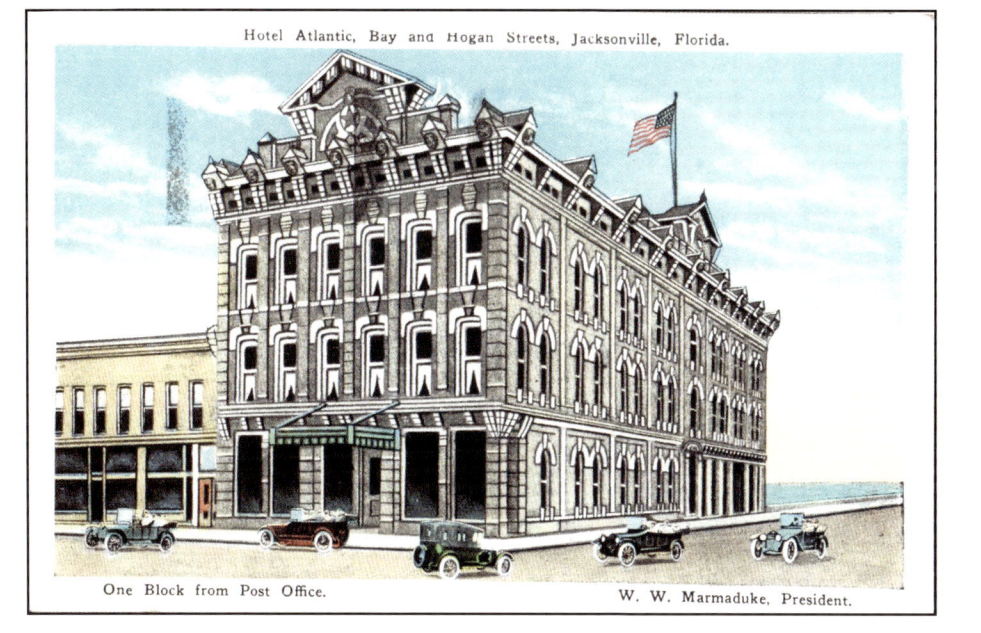
Hotel Atlantic, Bay and Hogan Streets, Jacksonville, Florida.

One Block from Post Office.   W. W. Marmaduke, President.

Hotel Burbridge
Jacksonville, Fla.

HOTEL MAYFLOWER, JACKSONVILLE, FLORIDA

Hotel George Washington, Jacksonville, Florida.

Burbridge Hotel.
The Burbridge Hotel, on the northeast corner of Forsyth and Clay Streets, opened in December 1911. The exterior of the 175-room hotel featured an enclosed balcony above the entrance. The lobby contained trophies of Ben Burbridge's hunting trips to Alaska and Africa. The seven-story hotel was particularly favored by traveling men and sportsmen. The hotel became the Floridian Hotel in 1942 and survived the wrecking ball until 1981. Circa 1910s, $5-7.

Mayflower Hotel.
The 250-room Mayflower Hotel, on the northwest corner of Bay and Julia streets, was formerly the Mason Hotel. It became the Mayflower in 1929 and was razed in January 1978 to become a parking lot. Circa 1930, $4-6.

George Washington Hotel.
The George Washington Hotel, on the northwest corner of Julia and Adams Streets, opened December 15, 1926. The fourteen-story hotel had "the innovation of a radio in every room." It became the first hotel in America to be completely air conditioned. It was destroyed in 1976 to make room for a parking lot. Circa 1920s, $4-6.

Hotel Carling, Jacksonville, Florida.

Carling Hotel.
The thirteen-story Carling Hotel, on the north side of Adams Street, between Laura and Main Streets, was built in 1926. Newspaper articles described the hotel as having "300 rooms with bath, running ice water, fans and the latest equipment in the rooms." Soon after Franklin D. Roosevelt was elected President in 1932, the Carling was renamed the Roosevelt Hotel. Circa 1920s, $4-6.

Elks Lodge.
The first Elks Club building was destroyed in the 1901 fire. The Elks Club shown here was razed in 1925 before construction of a third club building. Founded in 1891, Lodge 221 is the oldest Elks lodge in Florida. Cancelled 1906, $1-3.

TYPE OF GARAGE IN CAMP. CAMP JOHNSTON FLA

Camp Johnston.
In 1907 the city of Jacksonville bought land and gave it to the state to build Camp Joseph E. Johnston, a troop training center. The first state troops used the camp in 1909, and during World War I the camp became a quartermaster training post. After World War I, the camp was demobilized and buildings were taken down. A generation later, the site of Camp Johnston became the nucleus for Naval Air Station Jacksonville. Cancelled 1918, $6-8.

St. Johns River Ferry.
Before bridges were built, ferries were used to cross the St. Johns River from downtown Jacksonville to South Jacksonville. Shown is a view of the South Jacksonville ferry against the background of downtown Jacksonville. On April 2, 1922, the South Jacksonville ferry, with just one toot of her whistle, said farewell to her home waters and departed for Philadelphia to be used there as a ferryboat. Circa 1910s, $3-5.

WATER FRONT, FOOT OF MAIN STREET, JACKSONVILLE.

Dixieland Park.
Florida has many amusement parks; however, many more have come and gone. This view shows one of the first. Dixieland Park, the result of an ambitious effort to provide an all-around amusement center, opened in 1907. Located on the riverfront in Jacksonville, the park featured an arena of over four hundred wild animals, including eighty-seven lions, plus elephants and camels for children to ride. The park also had an ancient seventy-foot Live Oak tree that was often decorated in bright lights. Babe Ruth once played baseball at this park. Dixieland Park was a popular attraction that provided the people of Jacksonville and vicinity a place where entertainment, fairs, theatricals, athletics, and contests of every kind could be held. Cancelled 1912, $10-12.

Dixieland Park,
Jacksonville, Fla.

The Oriental Gardens.
Formerly an eighteen-acre private estate, Oriental Gardens, located on the banks of the St. Johns River, two miles South of downtown Jacksonville, was an early 1900s attraction of tropical and subtropical flowers, shrubs, and trees, and an entrancing Sunken Garden with small lakes and streams, bridges, fountains, and numerous Asiatic ornaments. Visitors could enjoy quiet, restful strolls along side mirror-like lagoons under the cool shade of towering Oak, Cypress, Pine, and other stately trees. Circa 1930s, $1-3.

Pablo Queen.
This view shows Pablo Queen, a 784 pound Alligator at the Florida Alligator Farm, on the South bank of St. Johns River. The farm was owned by H. I. Campbell, better known as "Young Alligator Joe." Circa 1910s, $3-5.

Ostrich Farm.
A view of several Ostriches at the Florida Ostrich Farm. The farm, on the south bank of St. Johns River, was owned by H. I. Campbell, who also owned a nearby Alligator Farm. Circa 1910s, $3-5.

Jacksonville's Favorite Oak Tree.
When Dixieland Park opened in 1907, this oak had already achieved a colossal size. Its majestic beauty and antiquity have awed visitors for many generations. This seventy-foot tall, twenty-five-foot trunk diameter Live Oak tree is now located in the Jessie Ball Dupont Park. Circa 1910, $1-3.

A Jacksonville Orange Grove.
The Citrus industry had its beginning in Florida about 1579 near St. Augustine, first settlement in America. By 1900, there were numerous groves in North and Central Florida. Shown is an orange grove in Jacksonville. Cancelled 1914, $1-3.

Pablo Beach.
This Duval County seaside community on the Atlantic Ocean is located just Southeast of Jacksonville. Named Pablo Beach after the Spanish form of Paul, Pablo Beach was incorporated in 1907. A paved highway leading from Jacksonville was built in 1910. Pablo Beach became Jacksonville Beach in 1925. Cancelled 1919, $3-5.

WATCHING THE BATHERS, PABLO BEACH, FLA.

AN EVERY DAY LINE UP OF AUTOMOBILES ON THE BEACH AT PABLO BEACH, FLA.

Automobiles on Pablo Beach.
In the early 1900s the entire section from Atlantic Beach to Ponte Vedra was the largest resort area in Northeast Florida. Tens of thousands of vacationers relaxed and played there during the summer; shown are some of them driving on Pablo Beach. Circa 1920s, $3-5.

U.S. Navy Bombers over the St. John's River

PLANES FROM OFFICIAL PHOTOGRAPH U. S. NAVY

Bombers over the St. Johns River.
This view shows U.S. Navy Bombers flying over St. Johns River during a World War II practice session. The skyline of Jacksonville can be seen in the background. Circa 1943, $2-4.

Palatka

An Early View of Palatka Waterfront. The St. Johns River, in the late 1880s, was teeming with Steamboats. Many of these boats were loaded with produce, citrus, and lumber, heading to Jacksonville. Other boats were slowly cruising the river with people on vacation, taking a trip up river to Silver Springs via the winding Ocklawaha River or just sight-seeing, enjoying the beauty and tranquility of the sparkling water and lush riverbanks. The town of Palatka had several hotels, homes, and businesses. Life in Palatka was good at this time and trains were just starting to enter the area. The Palatka waterfront was a busy port on the St. Johns River. Circa 1915, $10-12.

Water Front, Palatka, Fla.—5

Hiawatha Steamboat at the Palatka Landing.

During Florida's Steamboat Era (1830-1930), Palatka was a major river port on the St. Johns River, a popular tourist destination, and an important transshipment point. Its commercial history goes back to 1821 when it was founded as a trading post, taking its name from the Seminole Indian word meaning "ferry" or "crossing." Shown are two Steamboats tied up at the Palatka wharf. Copyright 1905, $15-17.

Photo. Only. Copyright 1905 by the Rotograph Co.
G 15673 "Hiawatha" at the Landing, Palatka, Fla.

Chapter Five

G 15657 Ocklawaha River Boat "Hiawatha" leaving Palatka, Fla.

Hiawatha Steamboat Leaving Palatka.
Palatka, the seat of Putnam County, is a town that still contains many reminders of its Golden Age (the Steamboat Era). Many of the antebellum structures have fallen on harder times, however, the St. Mark's Episcopal Church, used as barracks by Gen. Sherman's Union troops during the Civil War, is now a meticulously maintained, beautifully preserved reminder of the past. Circa 1906, $12-14.

Steamer "H. B. Plant" at A.C.L Dock, St. Petersburg, Fla.

H. B. Plant Steamboat.
The original *H. B. Plant* Steamboat carried mail, freight, and passengers to St. Johns River's settlements. The Steamboat was destroyed by fire in 1890. In 1899 a second *H. B. Plant* was built in Jacksonville. She may have served St. Johns River on local runs as she was a day boat, but in June 1901 she was sent to Tampa, to run on the Manatee River. This view shows the *H. B. Plant* at a St. Petersburg dock. The second *H. B. Plant* burned at a Tampa pier in 1913. Cancelled 1909, $7-9.

City Hall, Palatka, Fla.

City Hall.
The Palatka City Hall was built in 1905 at the corner of Reid and Second Streets. In 1961 the old Palatka Post Office became Palatka's City Hall. Circa 1907, $5-7.

Downtown Palatka.
City Hall, Saratoga Hotel, and the U.S. Post Office that opened
December 8, 1916. Circa 1920s, $4-6.

Putnam Hotel.
During the early 1880s Palatka's downtown area boasted many hotels.
The Arlington, Saratoga, Lafayette, Putnam, and others accommodated
as many as 6,000 visitors to Palatka. It was the most prosperous time
Palatka has ever known. Circa 1908, $5-7.

Arlington Hotel.
The Golden Age of tourism in Palatka flourished between the Civil War and
World War I, culminating in the 1880s. In 1884, one observer reported that
one hundred boats traveled between Jacksonville and Sanford or Enterprise
with Palatka considered the tourist town of Florida. This view shows the
Arlington, a popular hotel in the late 1880s. Cancelled 1914, $5-7.

James Hotel.
The James Hotel was located on the site of Palatka's first Masonic Hall,
which was later remodeled to become the Arlington Hotel. The Arlington
was demolished in 1916 and a more modern James Hotel was built on the
site in 1917. Circa 1918, $5-7.

71

Lemon Street looking E., Palatka, Fla.

Palatka, Fla. Dodge Street.

A Downtown Palatka Scene.
By 1870 Palatka was a thriving village with several stores, including a drug store, two churches, two steam mills, and two saw mills. Two large hotels (the Putnam House and St. Johns House) had opened to accommodate tourists. This view is of Lemon Street (now St. Johns Avenue) looking east toward the St. Johns River. Cancelled 1908, $12-14.

Street Scene.
A horse and buggy on Dodge Street. Circa 1907, $6-8.

Alligator Border Postcard.
A Lemon Street scene in downtown Palatka is illustrated in this Alligator Border postcard. The Alligator Border cards, published by S. Langsdorf and Company of New York and printed in Germany, are in great demand by collectors. Alligators were a novelty for northerners; Florida promoters got as much public relations mileage as possible from picturing them on the view cards. The Alligator Cards featured a trio of alligators, with a local scene inside the saurian border. It was a unique design and the quality of printing was excellent. Circa 1910, $30-100.

Street Scene.
A view of Fourth Street in Palatka. Circa 1908, $4-6.

73

Fourth Street, Palatka, Fla.

Fourth Street.
Another view of Fourth Street. Cancelled 1913, $2-4.

P-3   RUSTIC WATER-WHEEL AND SUSPENSION BRIDGE, RAVINE GARDENS, PALATKA, FLA.

4A-H2029

Ravine Gardens.
A collection of 95,000 azaleas, including sixty-four of the known seventy-two varieties of azaleas, that will live in an outdoor climate area contained in these gardens. Circa 1930s, $1-3.

P-5   VIEW FROM THIRD TERRACE, RAVINE GARDENS, PALATKA, FLA.

4A-H2024

Ravine Gardens.
A steep ravine was created during the Pleistocene Period (some 10,000 years ago) by water flowing from beneath the sandy ridges that flank the west shoreline of the St. Johns River. Through the ages, these ridges have shaped and re-shaped the ravines. Ravine Gardens, a histrionic example of this eroding force at work, is a natural wonder located at Palatka. The gardens, Palatka's most impressive attraction, opened in 1933 and were quickly hailed as "A New Wonder of the World." The gardens contained the single largest col-lection of azaleas in the world, 11,000 Palm trees, and more than 200,000 other subtropical plants. Circa 1930s, $1-3.

De Leon Springs

Chapter Six

Water Path to the St. Johns River.
The De Leon Springs forms a subterranean stream flowing approximately 94,000 gallons of water per minute, part of which is impounded in a pool like area. Excess water cascades over spillways into the spring run, called Spring Garden Creek. It then makes its way into Lake Woodruff, then Lake Dexter, and eventually flows into the St. Johns River, seven miles to the west. Under the boil at the main spring, a cavern extends to a depth of about twenty-eight feet. This leads to an underwater cave system that continues back into the limestone bedrock for about 170 feet. Cancelled 1906, $6-8.

Old Mill.
Native Americans may have occupied this area as early as 8,000 B.C. One of the oldest dugout canoes ever found in America was discovered here. After many years of Spanish and British hegemony, the springs became U.S. Territory in 1821. The Spring Garden Plantation owner, Orlando Rees, built a water wheel at the spring site to grind sugar cane. Seminole Indians sacked the plantation during the Second Seminole Indian War. The mill was later used to provide grain and supplies for Confederate forces in the Civil War. Circa 1915, $3-5.

Old Mill at De Leon Springs, near Daytona, Florida.

De Leon Springs near De Land, Fla.

Sugar Mill.
The Old Spanish Sugar Mill in De Leon Springs State Recreation Area (formerly Spring Garden Plantation) hasn't produced sugar in over 150 years. The mill, built previous to 1763, was burned by Seminole Indians in 1836. It was rebuilt, then burned again by Union soldiers during the Civil War after its machinery had been modified to make corn meal to feed Confederate troops. Cancelled 1909, $10-12.

Historic Ponce de Leon Springs
De Leon Springs, Fla.

Entrance to Springs.
This structure welcomes visitors to historic De Leon Springs Recreation Area (formerly Ponce De Leon Springs and Spring Garden Plantation), a major tourist attraction just north of DeLand. The statues of Ponce De Leon and the girl are symbolic of the historic background and glamour of the gardens. Behind them is a bas-relief map of the state. Circa 1930s, $1-3.

Boating in the Springs.
The serenity of the De Leon Springs is reflected in this view of several people boating in the spring. Cancelled 1909, $10-12.

De Leon Springs, Fla.

De Leon Springs, Fla. Outlet.

De Leon Springs, Fla. The Old Mill.

Spring Outlet.
The De Leon Springs still bubble forth the sulfur and minerals that nineteenth century boosters advertised as cures for "boils, fever sores, catarrh, kidney disease, asthma, nervous depression, rheumatism, erysipelas, etc." The mineral content of the water has apparently decreased in recent years, however, visitors still regard the spring as a Fountain of Youth in the sense of being a place for healthful outdoor recreation in a beautiful, natural setting. Cancelled 1910, $3-5.

Artifacts.
Thousands of Timucua Indian artifacts have been recovered from the springs by scuba divers, including many bone tools and ornaments, as well as objects for which their use is unknown. The bone artifacts are considered particularly valuable because in other climates and locations, bone does not survive as do pottery and stone. Cancelled 1910, $6-8.

77

THE SPRING, PONCE DE LEON SPRINGS, FLA.

Ponce De Leon Springs Inn.
In 1886 the name of Spring Garden was changed to De Leon Springs and tourists started arriving by railroad. A dam with a small outlet in it was installed to control the water in the pool. In 1927 an elaborate hotel was built at the site of the spring, and the boil was enclosed with cement in order to create a swimming pool. The hotel, called the Ponce De Leon Springs Inn, was the site of many parties and celebrations. The forty-room hotel was demolished in the 1960s. Circa 1920s, $7-9.

CASINO, PONCE DE LEON SPRINGS, FLA.

PONCE DE LEON SPRINGS, FLA.

Diving Tower.
The bath house and forty-five foot diving tower at De Leon Springs. Several years later, the tower was reduced to thirty feet for safer recreation. Circa 1920s, $7-9.

Donkey Rides.
This postcard shows a group of children on donkeys at De Leon Springs. Circa 1920s, $14-16.

FOR CHILDREN, PONCE DE LEON SPRINGS, FLA.

DeSoto House, DeLeon Springs, Fla.

DeSoto House.

In 1885, V. M. Bennett built the forty-room DeSoto House on the corner of Wheeler and Commerce Streets (the main street in De Leon Springs). A three-story frame building with porches on two sides, the hotel was built as a fishing resort and stopover for travelers. At the time, most people traveled to and from the area via Steamboat on the St. Johns River. Many pioneer settlers as well as visitors stayed at the hotel. Circa 1908, $8-10.

Real Photo Postcard.

View of De Leon Springs historical data. However, the claim that the springs were discovered by Don Juan Ponce De Leon is disputed. General Zachary Taylor, whose first name is misspelled on the postcard, was elected President in 1848. Circa 1910, $8-10.

Chimney.
A real photo postcard of the Sugar Mill chimney. Circa 1910, $3-5.

Gears and Chimney.
A real photo postcard of the Sugar Mill gears and furnace chimney. Circa 1910, $3-5.

Water Wheel.
Huge waterwheel of one of the oldest Sugar Mills in America. Circa 1940s, $3-5.

DeLand

Greetings from DeLand.
DeLand is known as the "Athens of Florida" for its interest in arts and education. In 1876, a manufacturer named Henry A. DeLand from Fairport, New York, met with local pioneers in the Pine woods on a sand ridge 3.5 miles east of the St. Johns River. They formed a town that was named for him. The city was incorporated in 1882. Circa 1940s, $3-5.

DeLand's Citrus Industry.
Since the nineteenth century, the DeLand area has been involved with the citrus industry; for many years it was DeLand's chief product and money crop. DeLand was once the heaviest shipping point for tangerines in the country. In the 1930s over a million and a quarter boxes of citrus fruit was picked and shipped annually from DeLand. Even today, DeLand is surrounded by producing orange groves. Circa 1915, $5-7.

Chapter Seven

Looking East on New York Avenue.
A view looking east from the College Arms Hotel on New York Avenue shows the delightfully shaded streets in a residential part of DeLand. Cancelled 1909, $6-8.

Water Surrounds DeLand.
The DeLand area has many beautiful and historic rivers, lakes, and springs: St. Johns, De Leon Springs, Gemini Springs, Blue Spring, Lakes Monroe and Woodruff, Hontoon Island, and Lake Helen. Circa 1908, $6-8.

Looking West on New York Avenue.
A view looking west on New York Avenue in front of present day St. Peter Catholic Church. Automobiles were beginning to show on DeLand's roads, but as seen in this postcard, horses and wagons still played a prominent role in getting around in DeLand. Circa 1907, $6-8.

Woodland Boulevard looking S., De Land, Fla.

Looking South on Woodland Boulevard.

Under Henry A. DeLand's direction, a street a mile long and sixty feet wide was cut through the woods and a row of trees planted down the middle. It was named Woodland Boulevard and bears little resemblance to the busy road that we know today. The trees were removed in 1915 when automobiles began replacing the horse and buggy. Cancelled 1918, $12-14.

Woodland Boulevard. DeLand, in 1888, had one of the nations earliest commercial street lighting systems (note the street light in this view of Woodland Boulevard). Three arc lights were installed on Woodland Boulevard and New York Avenue. They burned from sunset to midnight during the first years of operation. Circa 1907, $12-14.

Land, Fla. Woodland Boulevard.

Section of Business District,
De Land, Fla.

Downtown DeLand.
DeLand is a community reminiscent of an old-fashioned hometown, complete with a charming main street. This early view captured the traffic on Woodland Boulevard. Circa 1910s, $12-14.

Clara Avenue.
Rich in historic, cultural, and natural beauty, visiting DeLand is like stepping back to a more serene era. Shown is a view of Clara Avenue. The building on the right is the DeLand Public School, a wooden structure built in 1898. This view also shows an automobile and children's clothes of the era. Circa 1914, $6-8.

Automobiles on Woodland Boulevard.
Woodland Boulevard looking north from New York Avenue. Automobiles were beginning to show up in Deland, but as seen in this view, horses and wagons still played a prominent role in getting around in the city. Note the Buick car in the right foreground. The steeple of the First Presbyterian Church can be seen at the far end of the street on the left. Circa 1915, $12-14.

Volusia County Fair Grounds.
The Volusia County Fair Grounds were built on West New York Avenue near the railroad depot in 1925. By the year this postcard was mailed, the Volusia County Fair had become one of the largest county fairs in the southeast. Cancelled 1931, $12-14.

Volusia County Courthouse.
Opened in 1929, the historic copper dome of the Volusia County Courthouse in DeLand symbolizes freedom. Today, the historic courthouse has been replaced by a new modern courthouse (two blocks to the east); however, the historic courthouse is still open for public business. Circa 1930s, $2-4.

Dreka's Department Store, DeLand, Fla.

Volusia County Bank. De Land, Fla.

Dreka Department Store.
The Dreka Department Store building, completed in 1909, was George A. Dreka's second store (at the same location). It was the first reinforced concrete building constructed in Volusia County, and the oldest and largest example of the Mission style design in DeLand. This store later became a J. C. Penny store. The building is now the home of SouthTrust Bank. Cancelled 1912, $8-10.

Volusia County Bank.
This view shows the Volusia County Bank, a Classical Revival style building located on Woodland Boulevard. Circa 1910s, $8-10.

DeLand Public Library.
The DeLand Public Library, on the southwest corner of New York and Garfield Avenues, was founded in 1912. The sender of this real photo postcard wrote, "This building is opposite the Eastwood Hotel where my two elderly cousins are staying—so we are visiting the library." Circa 1930s, $10-12.

First National Bank Building, De Land, Fla.

PUBLIC SCHOOL, DELAND, FLA.

Public School.
The DeLand Public School was a wooden structure built in 1898 on the northwest corner of Clara and Rich Avenues. An addition to this school was constructed in 1907 that included fourteen classrooms and an auditorium that seated six hundred. Circa 1914, $6-8.

Country Club, De Land, Florida.

DeLand's First Skyscraper!
The First National Bank of DeLand, founded in 1910, was located in a small one-story brick structure. In 1924 the bank built the five-story structure shown in this view. The building contained twenty-eight offices in addition to the banking rooms. The year of 1929 spelled economic disaster for the entire nation. The First National Bank, like many others, closed its doors. The new Barnett National Bank of DeLand moved into the structure where it remained until 1954. Circa 1920s, $8-10.

Country Club.
A view of the DeLand Country Club that burned in the early 1930s and was rebuilt on the same site in the 1950s. Circa 1920s, $4-6.

De Land Memorial Hospital, De Land, Fla.—23

DeLand Memorial Hospital.
The DeLand Memorial Hospital, located on Wisconsin Avenue and North Stone Street, was built in 1920 to commemorate soldiers from DeLand who lost their lives in World War I. The structure, which embodies elements of the Colonial Revival and Mediterranean styles, is listed on the National Register of Historic Places. Today, the facility is a medical museum. Circa 1920s, $5-7.

DeLand High School.
In 1917, a brick building was built, at the same site as the wooden 1898 schoolhouse, for high school and elementary school children. During World War I, DeLand students assisted the war effort by planting gardens. Students also bought three Liberty Bonds at $50 each for the DeLand school by each bringing in five cents per month. In 1979, the building was destroyed by fire set by a student. Circa 1930s, $3-5.

DL-4—High School, Deland, Fla.

College Arms Hotel.
The College Arms Hotel, located at the corner of Amelia and New York Avenues, was one of Florida's grand hotels. At the turn of the twentieth century, when the hotel was in its prime, it had one of the state's few eighteen-hole golf courses. The course was kept trimmed by a flock of sheep. The hotel was demolished in 1949 to make room for Fish Memorial Hospital, which was demolished in 1997 to make room for a new Volusia County Courthouse. Circa 1912, $3-5.

Putnam Hotel.
The original wood-frame Putnam Inn, built in 1898, burned in 1917. In 1923 it was replaced by the still standing 150-room, Mediterranean Revival style Putnam Hotel on New York Avenue. The Putnam Hotel, still a landmark in downtown DeLand, is a reminder of days gone by. Circa 1920s, $3-5.

De Land Hotel, De Land, Florida.

AERIAL VIEW, STETSON UNIVERSITY, DELAND, FLA.

2891

DeLand Hotel.
The 100-room DeLand Hotel, located on South Woodland Boulevard, was built in 1926. An arcaded facade, parapet, pent roof with ceramic tiles, and stucco walls, contribute to its Mediterranean character. In the 1970s the hotel became the Landmark Hotel and in 1999 it was restored and adapted as a restaurant and hotel—the Artisan Inn. Circa 1920s, $8-10.

Stetson University.
An aerial view of Stetson University, established by Henry A. DeLand in 1886 as DeLand University, with the financial assistance of John B. Stetson, hat manufacturer. It was incorporated as a university under its present name in 1889. Most of the major buildings at Stetson University were built in the late 1880s or early 1900s. Today more than thirty buildings comprise the campus of the university. Circa 1920s, $4-6.

De Land Hall, Stetson University, De Land, Fla.

DeLand Hall.
DeLand Hall, the oldest academic building on the campus of Stetson University, is also the oldest building in Florida in continuous use for higher education purposes. It was a gift from city and academy founder Henry A. DeLand. This 1884 Second Empire-style designed building has been restored to its original "carpenter's Gothic" appearance. Cancelled 1909, $7-9.

Elizabeth Hall.
It may look like Independence Hall in Philadelphia, but this is Elizabeth Hall on the Stetson University campus in DeLand. It was built and given to the university by John B. Stetson in 1892. The architect was directed to design the building to resemble, as much as possible, Independence Hall in Philadelphia. Cancelled 1909, $7-9.

Science Hall.
In 1902, Henry M. Flagler financed the building of Science Hall at Stetson University, which housed an engineering program and Florida's first law school. Flagler's name was not associated with the building until after his death. Science Hall is now called Flagler Hall. Cancelled 1910, $5-7.

Hulley Tower.
Hulley Tower, a 116-foot tower containing an eleven-bell carillon, was built in 1934. It served as a mausoleum for Stetson's second president, Lincoln Hulley, and his wife, Eloise, for whom the chimes are named. The Eloise Chimes, first housed in the Elizabeth Hall tower in 1915, consisted of "rough cast" bells, four large and seven small ones, ranging from 575 to 3,000 pounds. Throughout the years the chimes have been in almost continuous use by Stetson music students, and traditionally were played at Commencement. Today only the lower portion of the tower remains. Circa 1930s, $3-5.

Chaudoin Hall.
Named for W. N. Chaudoin, a Stetson trustee from 1886 until his death in 1904, Chaudoin Hall also features Colonial Revival styling. The first part of the structure was built in 1892. Chaudoin Hall has many distinctive Dutch Revival features: an alpha-letter ("U") plan, a gambrel roof, multiple dormers, and a three-story silhouette. A small cupola with balustrade crowns the roof. Cancelled 1916, $4-6.

Library and Elizabeth Hall.
A view of the library (left) and Elizabeth Hall (right) on the campus of Stetson University. Elizabeth Hall was the first campus building that was wired for electricity when constructed in 1892. Cancelled 1914, $5-7.

DeLand Passenger Depot.
The Atlantic Coast Line Railroad Depot was completed in 1918. This depot is similar in design to the station in Green Cove Springs. Circa 1920s, $15-17.

Sanford

Steamboat Traffic on the St. Johns. The heyday of Steamboat traffic to Sanford was the years 1870-1930. In 1873 the *Volusia* Steamboat connected with the ox teams at Tuscawilla. In the 1880s the *Welaka* Steamboat left Jacksonville every Tuesday and Friday at 3 p.m. for Lake Jessup and intermediate landings, including Sanford. In 1885 the *Welaka* and the *Rosa* carried freight six days a week to Enterprise and Lake Jessup. On October 12, 1885, the *City of Jacksonville* (shown in this view) made the run from Jacksonville to Sanford in twelve and a half hours, the fastest trip on record. In 1887 an hourly ferry boat operated between Enterprise and Sanford. Circa 1908, $10-12.

Lake Monroe, Sanford, Florida

Steamboat on Lake Monroe. In the 1870s and 1880s the DeBary Merchants Line and then the DeBary-Baya Merchants Line served Sanford. In 1889 the Clyde Line bought the DeBary-Baya Line and continued service until 1930. Cancelled 1908, $3-5.

Lake Monroe, Florida

Clyde Line Steamboat Pier.
This view shows the Steamboat dock on Lake Monroe. Sanford, the best known of all the places on this part of St. Johns River, was celebrated as "The Celery City." Travelers stepping off a Steamboat or train in April, would be accosted by a smiling young woman asking, "Won't you try some of our celery?" Circa 1910, $10-12.

Steamboat Landing.
This view shows the Steamboat wharf in Sanford. The city's chief claim to fame is that it was once the center of a rich celery district that produced one-fifth of all the celery grown in this country. Circa 1906, $5-7.

Lake Monroe.
Going north from the Upper St. Johns, the river widens to form Lake Monroe, named in honor of the fifth U.S. President, James Monroe, in whose term Florida was acquired from Spain. The city of Sanford is on the lake's southern shore. Cancelled 1909, $5-7.

Overlooking the Steamboat Dock.
Sanford was founded in 1870 by General Henry B. Sanford, who also organized a land company, built a 600-foot pier into Lake Monroe, established telegraph service, and in 1875 erected the 200-room Sanford House. The hotel was torn down in 1920. Cancelled 1907, $5-7.

Steamer "City of Jacksonville" on Lake Monroe,
Sanford, Fla.

City of Jacksonville.
**This view shows the *City of Jacksonville* Steamboat on Lake Monroe near
Sanford. This was one of the largest Steamboats to sail on the St. Johns
River. Built in 1882, the *City of Jacksonville* was 160.5 feet long by 32.5
feet wide. This Steamboat had the longest life on the St. Johns. Her last
Clyde Line trip was in May 1928. Circa 1908, $16-18.**

Sanford Street Scene.
**Horse and buggy, automobiles, and a streetcar are shown
on this busy Sanford street. Circa 1910s, $8-10.**

St. Johns River View near Sanford, Fla.

A St. Johns River View.
Oak trees draped with Spanish Moss on the
St. Johns River near Sanford. Cancelled 1908,
$1-3.

Sanford, Fla. Lettuce Farm.

Lettuce Farm.
Although celery was the main agricultural crop grown in Sanford, lettuce was
also grown and shipped to northern cities. By the first decade of the twentieth
century, Sanford was one of the largest vegetable shipping centers in the United
States. Circa 1910, $6-8.

S-32—Park Avenue and Municipal Zoo from the Band Shell
on Lake Monroe, Sanford, Fla.

Sanford Zoo.
In 1925 the Sanford Zoo opened in
downtown Sanford along Lake Monroe. In 1973 the current Central Florida Zoo opened on U.S. Highway 17-92
in Sanford. Circa 1930s, $1-3.

Sanford House Hotel.
The Sanford House on Commercial Street stands decorated and waiting for the eagerly anticipated visit of President Grover Cleveland and his new bride March 27, 1889. Circa 1910s, $7-9.

S-5 — *Lemon Bluff, a Peaceful Rendezvous on the St. John's River near Sanford, Florida*

Lemon Bluff.
A peaceful view of the St. Johns River near Sanford. Circa 1930s, $1-3.

6B-H1228

97

O.5—THE CYPRESS METHUSELAH (SAID TO BE OVER 3,500 YEARS OLD), FLORIDA

THE "BIG TREE" ON U. S. 17 & 92, BETWEEN SANFORD AND ORLANDO, FLA.

Ex President and Mrs. Calvin Coolidge at dedication of Florida's "Big Tree" The Senator Cypress. Age 3500 years. Diameter 17½ ft. Circumference 47 ft. Height 126 ft. On U. S. 17 and 92 between Sanford and Orlando, Florida.

Big Bald Cypress Tree.
"The Senator" Cypress Tree is located on U.S. Highway 17-92, midway between Sanford and Orlando. It's the oldest Cypress tree in the United States, estimated to be 3,500 years or older. Circa 1930s, $1-3.

Cypress Tree Dedication.
Ex-President and Mrs. Calvin Coolidge at the dedication of "The Senator." It is located in Big Tree Park. Circa 1930s, $15-17.

Ocklawaha River

Chapter Nine

A Steamboat Trip up the Ocklawaha

D. Webster Dixon, the Vermont newspaperman who visited Florida in 1875 and 1876, wrote about his journey. The following are more of his accounts that appeared in his many columns published in the *St. Albans Messenger*.

There are four steamers making regular trips from Palatka to Silver Springs. These are the *Tuskawilla*, which carries the U.S. mail; the *Marion*, which has been in service some years; and the *Osceola* and *Okahumkee*. The last two are owned by Col. Hart. The *Osceola* is the best for passenger service. Each boat is a small stern-wheeler, about sixty feet in length and twenty-one feet wide, of light draft, and of course the cabin accommodations are not very extensive, but yet are comfortable. Leaving Palatka we sailed up the St. Johns twenty-five miles, where we entered the Ocklawaha opposite the growing town of Welaka. From this point to Silver Spring the distance is 110 miles.

For general description of the Ocklawaha, it is necessary to state that it is so named for one of the clans of the Seminoles who once flourished on its banks; it enters the St. Johns by a scarcely noticeable opening; it flows more than 300 miles, mainly through an unbroken forest of cypress and palmetto; its width varies from 23 to 75 feet, and its depth from 20 to 60 feet. The course of this river is as twisted as strands of a rope, and has turns so short as barely to allow the passage of a boat, frequently compelling the use of long poles to prevent the boat from running on shore. When two

COPYRIGHT-11-HARRIS. The Ocklawaha River, Florida.

Introducing the Ocklawaha.
The Ocklawaha River is one of Florida's major rivers. It is a tributary of the St. Johns River and, like St. Johns, flows northward. It is one of eight major rivers in the world that flows from south to north. The name is supposedly derived from the Timucua Indian word "Ockli-Waha," meaning "crooked river," or "great and winding river." The river consists of many hairpin turns, tortuous bends, narrow passageways, shallow areas, and many obstructions. Cancelled 1911, $3-5.

boats meet in one of these turns one must hug close to shore to give passage to the other. The trees that line the water's edge are frequently of very large size, and their branches interlace and arch the channel; sometimes a tree will fall across the river, obstructing navigation for several hours until its removal is effected by cutting away the trunk and branches. We viewed the passing scenery, keeping an eye out for alligators and snakes, with which we were told the river abounded.

As we proceeded we found that our way lay through a great cypress swamp, many of the trees being of gigantic size. Aquatic plants bordered each shore, and silvery moss and other parasites draped the tall trees in fantastic shapes. Here and there the river is so narrow that the smaller branches of the trees rake the sides of the boat, and force persons on deck to change their positions rather suddenly.

We reached the Silver Spring Creek (now called the Silver River) or "Run" as it is called by the natives, 102 miles from the mouth of the river. Here we left the Ocklawaha, and proceeded a distance of eight miles up the "Run" to the famous spring. The "Run" is a hundred yards wide and from 15 to 25 feet deep; and so clear is the water that the bottom is distinctly visible everywhere. Thus we could see the fish both great and small, hundreds of turtles, and a great variety of marine plants as plainly as if they were at the surface. The bottom of the "Run" seemed to be composed of limestone and pebbles, reflecting colors like silver and emerald. Finally, we reached the spring, an almost circular basin 125 feet wide. Here we made a landing and a stay of three hours. We found two other steamers making ready for the return trip. Silver Springs cannot be called a large place; there is a small hotel, two stores, and half a dozen dwellings. It is five miles from here to Ocala, with which there is stage communication.

On the Ocklawaha River. "The Ocklawaha is the sweetest water lane in the world, a lane which runs for more than 150 miles of pure delight," wrote poet Sidney Lanier in 1876. (It is actually recorded to be 130 miles long.) It is the largest tributary of the St. Johns River. Circa 1908, $3-5.

On the Oklawaha River, Florida.

The water (in the spring) is marvelously transparent, so that the minutest object on the bottom can be easily distinguished. There are several springs in different parts of the basin, the water flowing in from some subterranean reservoir. At the spring where the greatest quantity of water flows, the upward current is strong enough to carry a large stone a distance of twenty-five feet before it touches bottom. A somewhat startling feature is presented when we pass over the transparent water in a small boat, in the sunlight. Then it seems as if you were suspended in mid air, the boat and its occupants being reflected in the depths of the basin, and producing a miraculous appearance.

After inspecting the natives and dogs of the place we were prepared to leave. Our boat got underway for the return trip to Palatka, which is made four or five hours quicker than the ascending voyage. On reaching the Ocklawaha again we saw some lighters, or flatboats, tied at shore, which had descended from the river above the "Run." The steamers do not attempt to navigate the river beyond this point; formerly they went up as far as a landing called Okeehumkee, near which there are lakes of considerable extent, yet the passage was so slow, and beset with numerous obstructions, that this portion of the route was finally abandoned. Below these lakes, in a comparatively unsettled region, there are other lakes called by such beautiful Indian names as Ichepucksassa, Tohopekaliga, and Okliakonkee, and rivers with such refreshing names as Tsalapopkahatchee, Tahkatchochee and Elotsateehowethla. I don't suppose you would care to print many of these names every day. It may be apprehended that the person who should pronounce one of these names correctly might not survive the mental strain.

Scene on the Ocklawaha, Florida

Along the Charming Ocklawaha River.

In 1900, the Ocklawaha River was still untamed. The northern section wound its way through a vast cypress and hardwood bottomland forest from Silver Springs to St. Johns. South of the Silver River, the dense swamp forests gave way to broad, flat sawgrass prairies through which the river meandered from its headwaters in Central Florida's Chain of Lakes. Cancelled 1910, $3-5.

Picturesque Ocklawaha River, Florida.

Picturesque Ocklawaha River. General Ulysses S. Grant, on his return from a tour of the world, pronounced the Ocklawaha River the most charming of rivers, and this trip one of the most pleasing events of his life. Circa 1920s, $1-3.

Osceola's Last Battlefield. One of the loveliest spots along the Ocklawaha River is a grassy knoll with Pine trees growing on it. About thirty-four miles north of this spot, on the Ocklawaha, is Payne's Landing, where the first treaty with the Seminole Indians was signed about 1833—to be broken by Osceola, the famed leader, in 1835. Circa 1910, $6-8.

COPYRIGHT-11-HARRIS.

Chief Osceola's Last Battlefield along the Ocklawaha River, Florida.

Ocklawaha River Trip to Silver Springs.
Palatka was the starting point of the Ocklawaha River steamers. Going south on St. Johns River for twenty-five miles, they entered the old forests of the "crooked river," which is the English translation of its name. The journey ended at Silver Springs, one hundred and ten miles farther on. This view shows the narrowness of the river in places where it is little more than a creek. Steamboat passengers often wondered if the boat would be obligated to retreat. Circa 1908, $10-12.

Steamer Entering the Narrow Oklawaha River, Florida.

Metamora Steamer Entering the Ocklawaha River.
Steamboats from Palatka enter the Ocklawaha River across St. Johns River from the town of Welaka. As shown in this view of the *Metamora*, the boatload of passengers was on deck looking forward to a thrilling trip on this popular river. Cancelled 1913, $18-20.

Deep Creek.
In 1890, William Henry Jackson, a commercial landscape photographer, photographed a small steamer plowing through the mist toward a lone silhouetted figure in a skiff on the narrow reaches of Deep Creek, a tributary of the St. Johns River. Postcard publishers used this photograph on several Florida river postcards, including the Ocklawaha. Circa 1907, $7-9.

Right: A Private Mailing Card. The Private Mailing Card Era was 1898-1901. On May 19, 1898, private printers were granted permission to print and sell cards that bore the inscription "Private Mailing Card." They are called PMCs. The use of the word "Postcard" was granted by the government to private printers December 24, 1901. Copyright 1901, $10-12.

Right: Ocklawaha River Wildlife. The diverse landscape of the Ocklawaha River area provides habitat and feeding for a variety of wildlife species, such as Alligators, Black Bears, Wolves, Panthers, Razorback Hogs, Turtles, Wild Turkeys, Bobcats, Deer, Otter, Foxes, Raccoons, Skunks, Armadillos, Sandhill Cranes, Egrets, Herons, and numerous waterfowl species. Wildlife was plentiful in the early days of settlement. Cancelled 1914, $3-5.

THE BEAUTIFUL OCKLAWAHA RIVER, NEAR SILVER SPRINGS, FLORIDA

Voyaging on the Ocklawaha.
Travel writers explored Florida in the late 1800s with the same zest they now display for Europe, the Caribbean, South America, and Mexico. The Ocklawaha River and Silver Springs offered the combined lure of remoteness and the romance of vanished Indian days. Even the names Hubbard Hart gave his Steamboats added to the charm—*Ocklawaha, Okeehumkee, Osceola, Astatula, Tuskawilla,* and *Hiawatha.* Circa 1920s, $2-4.

ALONG THE CHARMING OCKLAWAHA RIVER, FLORIDA

Ocklawaha River, Fla. Running Log Rafts.

Running Log Rafts.
Huge stands of Cypress and Cedar were cut and rafted down Ocklawaha River to a point on St. Johns, where they were loaded on schooners and sent to Jacksonville and other points north. Cancelled 1912, $14-16.

The Randall Hotel on the
Ocklawaha River at Connor, Fla.

P.T. Randall's Orange Grove.
The Randall Orange Grove and Hotel, located at Conner Landing on the Ocklawaha River, was a favorite stop for Steamboat passengers. Cancelled 1915, $14-16.

A Ferry on the Ocklawaha River.
This view shows an old ferry at Grahamville, a community founded on the Ocklawaha River by John Conner Graham soon after the Second Seminole War (1835-1842). The raft was attached to a loop of cable run through pulleys on opposite banks of the narrow river. An engine on a nearby shore drove the cable. Copyright 1902, $12-14.

Tourists by the Hart Line Steamers are permitted to visit
P. T. Randall's Orange Grove at Conner Landing,
Ocklawaha River, Florida.

Conner Landing.
Passengers of the *Hiawatha* Steamboat visiting the Randall Orange Grove. This river port, located two miles from Grahamville, served as a popular terminal for Ocklawaha River traffic. Circa 1904, $18-20.

Ocklawaha River, Fla. Florida Crackers and House boat.

Florida Crackers and Houseboat.
In the 1800s most people found that Florida crackers lived a primitive way of life, however, they also found the crackers were generous, hospitable, unassuming, and friendly toward strangers. The children were as natural as wild animals, yet disciplined and respectful of their elders. Cancelled 1908, $8-10.

A 13642 The Ferry, Grahamville on the Ocklawaha River, Fla.

Grahamville Ferry.
A ferry on the Ocklawaha River. Circa 1904, $8-10.

On the Ocklawaha River, Fla.

Astatula Steamboat on the Ocklawaha.
One passenger in 1902 stated, "The visitor to Florida, who misses a trip up the Ocklawaha River on one of the famous river Steamboats of the Hart Line, fails to behold the greatest attraction of the state." Circa 1904, $18-20.

Hiawatha Steamboat.
Hubbard L. Hart moved to Florida from Vermont in 1854. He soon realized the potential for Steamboat service to the headwaters of Silver Springs. Hart Line Steamboats did a brisk business bringing in tourists from Palatka on the St. Johns River. The largest boat in the Hart Line was the *Hiawatha*, shown here. It was the last of the great Ocklawaha steamers. Circa 1907, $18-20.

SCENE ON THE OCKLAWAHA RIVER, FLORIDA.

Orange Boat.
The first Ocklawaha River steamers were primarily freight carriers, but a growing influx of tourists and travelers in the years following the Civil War (1861-65) led to modifications that accommodated passengers as well as cargo. Shown is a Steamboat loaded with boxes of oranges. Circa 1908, $18-20.

IN FLORIDA. Orange Boat on the Ocklawaha River.

Nighttime Run.

The nighttime run up the Ocklawaha River from Palatka to Silver Springs offered one of the most beautiful sights in Florida, as the pitch-pine torches placed atop the pilot house of the Steamboat threw a light upon the dense vegetation of the shore. This view shows the *Hiawatha* of the Hart Line. Circa 1909, $18-20.

"THE ILLUMINATED OCKLAWAHA FOREST," A WEIRDLY BEAUTIFUL RADIANCE.

Okeehumkee Steamboat on the River.

The *Okeehumkee* Steamboat was built for Hubbard L. Hart's Steamboat company (Hart Line) at Palatka in 1873. The boat was 84.4 feet long, 21.4 feet wide, and was powered by a 150 horsepower steam engine. Copyright 1901, $10-12.

Steamboats' A' Coming!
The *William Howard* Steamboat cautiously pokes her way through the dense foliage on the Ocklawaha River. This steamer, along with the *Mary Howard* and *Sophie Howard*, were owned by Captain Hatten Howard. Cancelled 1912, $18-20.

UP THE OKLAWAHA RIVER, FLORIDA.

Okeehumkee Steamboat.
Okeehumkee's recessed stern wheel throws out water as she proceeds on her Ocklawaha River journey. This view shows the *Okeehumkee* easing her way toward Silver Springs. Note the closeness of the bordering trees and aquatic vegetation. The crooked labyrinthian channel of the Ocklawaha River required expertise in the pilot house of a Steamboat, and no tourist who had made the trip on the river doubted the statement of one Steamboat captain that he had counted 976 angles and horseshoe turns in the famous river. Copyright 1902, $10-12.

Silver Springs

Silver River.

This stream with its mirror-like waters navigable for large Steamboats is the overflow of the mysterious Silver Springs and is seven miles in length from Silver Springs to where it unites with the Ocklawaha River. Its current is very swift from the gushing springs along its headwaters, making it hard work for the steamers to push around the numerous turns. Great beds of rock and shell formation, bordered by various colored mosses, shoot upward a great body of boiling eddying crystal water over which the steamers glide with difficulty. Circa 1911, $5-7.

Silver River/Silver Springs.

The Silver River originates from the largest artesian spring in Florida. The bowl of Silver Springs is four hundred feet in diameter and reaches depths of forty feet. It flows at a rate of 530 million gallons per day from the artesian openings in the underground aquifer. The spring is believed to be over 25,000 years old. The Silver River is an important tributary of the Ocklawaha River, which feeds the St. Johns River. The flora and fauna along the banks of the crystal clear water of Silver Springs and the Silver River provide a spectacle—weird, wondrous, and magical—to be remembered as one of the great experiences in a lifetime. In 1845 James Rogers purchased eighty acres surrounding Silver Springs for $1.25 per acre. Silver Springs became a center for commerce and tourism. Stagecoaches, Steamboats, railroads, and highways all went by the Springs. Circa 1930s, $3-5.

Chapter Ten

Bird's Eye View.
This aerial view shows both Silver Springs and the Silver River. The springs has attracted scientists and scholars from the world over as much for its natural beauty as the opportunity it offers for study and research in fields ranging from archeology and paleontology to geology and botany. Cancelled 1936, $1-3.

AIRPLANE VIEW OF SILVER SPRINGS, FLA.

5A-H1375

Steamboat Arriving at Silver Springs.
In the late 1800s and early 1900s it was "the thing" for tourists and wealthy Florida landowners to go on the Hart Line Steamboats to the fancy resort at Silver Springs. Thousands of visitors each year rode the picturesque Ocklawaha River Steamboats to the springs as Northeast Florida tourism boomed in those fabulous years. Shown is the *Okeehumkee* Steamboat arriving at the Silver Springs dock. Cancelled 1913, $18-20.

General View on the Ocklawaha River, Florida

542-75

Freight and Passenger Boats at Landing, Silver Springs, near Ocala, Fla.

Boats at the Silver Springs Landing.
Shown, the *G.A. Carmichael* and the *City of Ocala* tied up at the Silver Springs dock. Other boats owned by C. Ed Carmichael were the *Wekiva* and the *Silver Springs*. The *G.A. Carmichael* was built especially for the river trade and at the time was the largest freight boat in operation on the Ocklawaha River. Cancelled 1921, $8-10.

Steamer "Hiawatha" at Silver Springs, near Ocala, Fla.

Hiawatha Steamboat at Silver Springs.
In the early 1900s, the *Hiawatha* left Palatka on Mondays, Wednesdays, and Fridays at 12:30 p.m., or on arrival of trains from Jacksonville, St. Augustine, Miami, and Tampa, and arrived at Silver Springs before noon the next day. Return trips left Silver Springs on Tuesdays, Thursdays, and Saturdays afternoon, arriving at Palatka the next morning. Circa 1908, $14-16.

Photo. Only. Copyright 1905 by the Rotograph Co.
G 15686 At the Landing, Silver Springs, Fla.

Okeehumkee Steamboat at Silver Springs.
Silver Springs was a tourist attraction over 150 years ago. The *Okeehumkee* brought visitors up the St. Johns, Ocklawaha, and Silver Rivers before 1850. The fare from Palatka to Silver Springs, including meals and berth, was $7. Shown is the *Okeehumkee* on an overnight trip to Silver Springs. Copyright 1905, $22-24.

COPYRIGHT-11 HARRIS.

On the largest Spring of Silver Springs,
Marion County, Fla.

HIAWATHA

HART LINE

HIAWATHA

Hiawatha Arriving at Silver Springs.
In 1873, William Bryant, author, poet and editor of one of the most influential newspapers in America, visited the springs and thought they were like "a well of transparent water… so clear you see at great depth the fish with which they abound." Circa 1911, $22-24.

The Freight Depot, Silver Springs,
near Ocala, Fla.

The Freight Depot.
In 1875 the village of Silver Springs consisted of a wharf, warehouses, a turpentine distillery, and country stores with an assortment of goods— clothes, fiddles, groceries, school books, and a tavern. A stage line operated out of Silver Springs three times a week to Ocala, Gainesville, Brooksville, and Tampa. Circa 1912, $6-8.

6221. SILVER SPRINGS ON THE OCKLAWAHA, FLA.   COPYRIGHT, 1902, BY DETROIT PHOTOGRAPHIC CO

Early View of Silver Springs.
Pictured: two women in sunbonnets in a glass bottom rowboat at
Silver Springs. Copyright 1902, $12-14.

Boating on Silver Springs, Florida

Boating.
This view shows young couples enjoying the underwater beauty of
the spring. The glass bottom boat was invented by a local youth,
Philip Morrell, in a crude rowboat. In 1878, Hullam Jones built an
advanced version and began rowing visitors around the springs for
a fee. Cancelled 1907, $12-14.

SEEING SILVER SPRINGS IN GLASS BOTTOM BOATS, OCALA, FLA.

Early Glass Bottom Boat.
While on glass bottom boats, myriad of fish can be seen, including
catfish, shad, needlefish, eels, warmouth, shellcrackers, mullet,
bream, largemouth bass, and huge gars. Some thirty-six varieties live
in the springs and river. Snakes, alligators, and turtles also may be
seen lying on the banks of the Silver River. Circa 1920s, $6-8.

Seeing Silver Springs in Glass Bottom Boats

Glass Bottom Boats.
A view of Silver Springs and glass bottom boats. Circa 1913,
$2-4.

SILVER SPRINGS FLORIDA

© H. R. Bezant

"LOOKING INTO NATURE'S UNDER WATER FAIRYLAND" THROUGH GLASS BOTTOM BOAT ON MAMMOTH SPRING

Underwater Viewing at Silver Springs.
This is one of the most popular attractions at the park. Passengers sit on benches arrayed around a center glass section in the middle of the boat while the captain gives an informative discourse on the history and nature of Silver Springs. Circa 1920s, $6-8.

933   FEEDING FISH FROM GLASS BOTTOM BOAT AT SILVER SPRINGS, FLA.

V 18458

6A-H595

Feeding the Fish.
Visitors are offered a chance to feed the fish while riding on a glass bottom boat. Circa 1920s, $3-5.

The Fish Play "Football" at Florida's Silver Springs

18

Underwater Football.
Visitors get a close look at the playful fish. Circa 1930s, $2-4.

BATHING IN THE CRYSTAL CLEAR WATERS AT SILVER SPRINGS, FLA.

PHOTO BY REVELS

3A469

Growth at Silver Springs.
In 1898 H. L. Anderson, an Ocala lawyer, purchased Silver Springs and surrounding land. In 1909, C. Ed Carmichael obtained title to the eighty acres around the springs from Anderson. Carmichael began improving the Glass Bottom Boats; however they were still oar-powered. W. M. Davidson and Carl Ray, Sr., in 1924, leased the springs for fifty years. The following year gasoline motors were installed in the Glass Bottom Boats. In 1932 these were supplanted by electric motors. Over the years, many new features were added at the springs and in 1950, over 800,000 visitors enjoyed its natural beauty. Silver Springs had become an international attraction. Cancelled 1935, $10-12.

Jungle Cruise on Tropical Silver River at Florida's Silver Springs

Jungle Cruise.
The seven mile Jungle Cruise on the Silver River provided visitors with an excellent view of the "Real Florida." Circa 1930s, $2-4.

WATER NYMPHS AT SILVER SPRINGS, OCALA, FLA. "IN THE KINGDOM OF THE SUN".

105782

Water Nymphs.
Fish and turtles weren't the only game to enjoy the crystal clear waters of Silver Springs. Circa 1930s, $10-12.

Feeding the Monkeys.
Several troops of wild Rhesus and South American Golden Squirrel monkeys lived in the trees along the banks of the Silver River. These monkeys, exotic to the region, were introduced in the 1930s by Colonel Tooey, the Jungle Cruise promoter. Today, about five hundred monkeys live in the area. This is the only tribe of monkeys living wild in the United States. The monkeys always put on a good show. Skippers of the Silver Springs Jungle Cruise boats would stop and feed the monkeys. Circa 1940s, $1-3.

A Cruise to Silver Springs.
This cruise starts on Lake Dora. The trip goes through the Chain of Lakes that lead to Silver Springs. Then, the boat enters the Dora Canal, a setting unsurpassed in beauty. A little farther, after the boat leaves Lakes Eustis and Griffin, it enters the Ocklawaha River. After the boat passes the locks at Moss Bluff, the boat skipper informs passengers that the jungle will be thicker, many beautiful birds will be seen, also snakes, alligators, and turtles, all of which add interest to the trip. Everyone is fascinated as the dark waters of the Ocklawaha River change to the clear crystal water of the Silver River. After a seven mile ride up the Silver River the boat arrives at the Silver Springs dock. Circa 1940s, $2-4.

Old Cannibal.
This seven-hundred pound, twelve-foot long alligator was exhibited in a natural habitat pen at Silver Springs. Circa 1930s, $3-5.

Fish and Wildlife

Chapter Eleven

Alligators.
In the early 1800s many visitors to Florida amused themselves by shooting Alligators from the deck of a Steamboat. Even John J. Audubon, an early nineteenth century naturalist, found Alligator hunting to be suitable entertainment for tourists. Regional guidebooks pointed out the best spots for Alligator hunting. Commercial hunting and poaching became widespread throughout Florida as Alligator skins became popular for a wide variety of leather items. Today, Alligator hunting is controlled and Alligators are plentiful on the St. Johns River. Cancelled 1909, $3-5.

Miss Alli-Gator, Florida

Wildlife on the St. Johns River.
In the 1800s, animal life along the river was plentiful. Visitors to the river would see Herons, Ducks, Eagles, and other bird life. Alligators, Turtles, Deer, Boars, and other animals could often be seen on the banks of the river. Tourists could travel on Steamboats for about $5 per trip. Fish were caught as the boat traveled, and passengers had them that night for dinner. Menus on some Steamboats included all kinds of fresh vegetables, oranges, and grapefruit just off the trees. If a Cabbage Palm was handy, they would stop the boat, and a crew member would cut the green tender tip; Northerners liked the heart of the Cabbage Palm. They also liked Wild Turkey, chicken, venison, and quail. At most Steamboat stops farmers and hunters were waiting to sell Game and Birds. Copyright 1913, $1-3.

Wild Ducks on a Florida River where Hunting is good.

A Native of Florida

Florida's Favorite Reptile.
Alligators can often be seen on the banks of the St. Johns River. Alligators in the wild are believed to live thirty-five to fifty years. In captivity their life span may be significantly longer, perhaps sixty to 100 years. If the Florida Alligator wanted to trace its family tree, it could go back ten million years. Circa 1908, $2-4.

A Florida Manatee.

Manatee.
For millions of years the Manatee has lived in Florida's rivers, springs, and swamps. They are found in all areas of St. Johns River. During the winter months many of St. Johns River Manatees migrate to the warm waters of Blue Spring, near Orange City. Circa 1910, $10-12.

New Smyrna, Fla. Old Spanish Shell Mound.

Early Inhabitants.
The only physical records we have of the earliest inhabitants of St. Johns River are the shell mounds and the implements they contain. Shell mounds parallel St. Johns for about three-quarters of its course. Found in these mounds have been pottery, human skeletons, weapons, ornaments, and food remains. Popular food for the early Indians was oysters, clams, crabs, and other shell animals. Circa 1910, $6-8.

Bird Hunting on the St. Johns.
A variety of wild birds and animals attracted hunters to St. Johns. The Upper St. Johns was referred to as a fisherman's and hunter's heaven. Cancelled 1914, $1-3.

Bird Life on the St. Johns.
White Ibis, Limpkins, Pelicans, Wood Ibis, Ducks, Snowy Egrets, Purple Gallinule, Whooping Cranes, Snowy Heron, Bittern, Eagles, Osprey, Blue Herons, and many other birds are plentiful on the St. Johns River. A Great Blue Heron is shown in this view. Circa 1910, $4-6.

Fine Sport,
Boating and
Fishing,
Florida.

Fishing at Mayport, Fla.

Fishing at Mayport.
Mayport, situated at the mouth of St. Johns River, is a fishing village, and home to U.S. Navy aircraft carriers. It's also the home port for one of the large north Florida shrimp fishing fleets. This early view shows a boatload of people fishing in the St. Johns at Mayport. Circa 1908, $4-6.

O-19—Ocala National Forest,
"The Sportsman's Paradise," Ocala, Fla.

Boating.
Many people living on or near St. Johns River depended on the river for food and livelihood. Circa 1908, $3-5.

A Sportsman's Paradise.
The Ocala National Forest is a national forest founded on the north and part of the west side by the Ocklawaha River and on the east side by St. Johns. Fishing is great in this area of the St. Johns River as well as in many other locations along the river. Circa 1930s, $1-3.

A Fine Catch of Fish.
The waters of Upper St. Johns River and the numerous lakes it links together were teeming with bass, pickerel, perch, and other varieties of fish. Circa 1920s, $3-5.

Shad Fishermen.
A view of an 1890 Ensminger Brothers photograph showing shad fishermen bringing their catch of fish to the Sanford dock. Circa 1910s, $8-10.

Bass Fishing.
Bass fishing is popular in all areas of the St. Johns River. Copyright 1911, $1-3.

A Good Days Catch, Florida.

Happy Fishermen.
A good day's catch.
Cancelled 1919. $3-5.

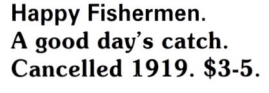

Bibliography

A Guide To Florida's St. Johns River. Sanford, Florida: Rivership Romance, 1988.

Alvers, Nancy Cooley and Janice Smith Mahaffey. *Our Place In Time: A Chronology of Putnam County*. Palatka, Florida: Palatka Printing Company, 1995.

Alvers, Nancy Cooley, Cora Solana Middleton, and Janice Smith Mahaffey. *San Mateo: God's Country*. Palatka, Florida: Palatka Printing Company, 1993.

Belleville, Bill. *River of Lakes: A Journey On Florida's St. Johns River*. Athens, Georgia: The University of Georgia Press, 2000.

Bennett, Charles E. *Twelve on the River St. Johns*. Jacksonville, Florida: University of North Florida Press, 1989.

Blanchard, Fessenden S. *A Cruising Guide to the Inland Waterway and Florida*. New York, New York: Dodd, Mead & Company, 1954.

Cabell, Branch and A. J. Hanna. *The St. Johns: A Parade of Diversities*. New York, New York: Farrar & Rinehart, Inc., 1943.

Carlson II, Charlie C. *When Celery Was King*. New Smyrna Beach, Florida: Carlson Family of Florida, 1997.

Carstarphen, Dee. *Narrow Waters*. Wicomico Church, Virginia: Pen and Ink Press, 1998.

Clark, Susan. *A Historic Tour Guide of Palatka and Putnam County, Florida*. Palatka, Florida: Putnam County Historical Society, 1992.

Crooks, James B. *Jacksonville After The Fire, 1901-1919*. Jacksonville, Florida: University of North Florida Press, 1991.

Davis, Frederick T. *History of Jacksonville, Florida and Vicinity, 1513-1924*. St. Augustine, Florida: The Florida Historical Society, 1925.

DeLand, Helen Parce. *Story of DeLand and Lake Helen, Florida*. DeLand, Florida: Louis H. Walden, 1928.

Dreggors, William J., Jr. *St. Johns River: The Steamboat Era* (video). DeLand, Florida: West Volusia Historical Society, 1997.

Dreggors, William J., Jr. and John Stephen Hess. *A Century of West Volusia County, 1860-1960*. DeLand, Florida: West Volusia Historical Society, 1993.

A Pictorial History of West Volusia County, 1870-1940. DeLand, Florida: West Volusia Historical Society, 1989.

Fitzgerald, T. E. *Historical Highlights of Volusia County*. Daytona Beach, Florida: The Observer Press, 1939.

Volusia County Past and Present. Daytona Beach, Florida: The Observer Press, 1937.

Francke, Jr., Arthur E. *Early Days Of Seminole County, Florida*. Sanford, Florida: Seminole County Historical Commission, 1984.

DeBary Conversations. DeBary, Florida: DeBary Hall, Inc., 1990.

Francke, Jr., Arthur E., Alyce Hockaday Gillingham, and Maxine Care Turner. *Volusia The West Side*. DeLand, Florida: West Volusia Historical Society, 1986.

Gallant Gene. *Riverboats A'Coming!: The Colorful Era of Riverboating on the Ocklawaha and Silver Rivers*. Ocala, Florida: SRM Publications, 1994.

Goggin, John M. *Space and Time Perspective in Northern St. Johns Archeology, Florida*. Gainesville, Florida: University Press of Florida, 1998.

Gold, Pleasant Daniel. *History of Volusia County, Florida*. DeLand, Florida: Self-published, 1927.

Gotschall, Phil and Fred Allen. *Healing Waters: A History of DeLeon Spring*. DeLeon Springs, Florida: Friends of De Leon Springs State Park, Inc., date unknown.

Graff, Mary B. *Mandarin on the St. Johns*. Gainesville, Florida: University of Florida Press, 1953.

Hebel, Ianthe Bond. *Centennial History of Volusia County, Florida 1854-1954*. Daytona Beach, Florida: College Publishing Company, 1955.

Hollis, Tim. *Glass Bottom Boats & Mermaid Tails*. Mechanicsburg, Pennsylvania: Stackpole Books, 2006.

Into Tropical Florida. Jacksonville, Florida: DeBary-Baya Merchants' Line, 1884.

Jacksonville Historical Society. *Jacksonville In Vintage Postcards*. Charleston, South Carolina: Arcadia Publishing, 2001.

La Fleur, Joan J., Editor. *Our Story of Orange City, Florida, Fourth Edition*. Orange City, Florida: Village Improvement Association, Inc., Orange City Woman's Club, 2000.

Lycan Gilbert L. *Stetson University: The First 100 Years*. DeLand, Florida: Stetson University Press, 1983.

Marth, Del and Marty Marth. *The Rivers of Florida*. Sarasota, Florida: Pineapple Press, Inc., 1990.

McCarthy, Kevin M. *St. Johns River Guidebook*. Sarasota, Florida: Pineapple Press, 2004.

Michaels, Brian E. *The River Flows North*. Palatka, Florida: Putnam County Archives and History Commission, 1976.

Milanich, Jerald T. *Florida Indians and the Invasion from Europe*. Gainesville, Florida: University Press of Florida, 1995.

Mitchell, C. Bradford. *Paddle-Wheel Inboard: Some of the History of Ock-*

lawaha River Steamboating and of the Hart Line. Providence, Rhode Island: The Steamboat Society of America, 1983.

Mueller, Edward A. *Along The St. Johns and Ocklawaha Rivers*. Charleston, South Carolina: Arcadia Publishing, 1999.

Ocklawaha River Steamboats. Jacksonville, Florida: Self-published, 1983.

Steamboating on the St. Johns: 1830-1885. Melbourne, Florida: South Brevard Historical Society.

Steamships of the Two Henrys. Jacksonville, Florida: Self-published, 1996.

St. Johns River Steamboats. Jacksonville, Florida: Self-published, 1986.

Mueller, Edward A. and Barbara A. Purdy. *The Steamboat Era In Florida*. Gainesville, Florida: University of Florida, 1985.

Snodgrass, Dena. *Jacksonville: A Brief History*. Jacksonville, Florida: The Florida Times-Union, 1968.

Spencer, Donald D. *A Postcard Journey Along the St. Johns River*. Ormond Beach, Florida: Camelot Publishing, 2002.

Around DeLand: A Postcard History. Ormond Beach, Florida: Camelot Publishing, 2001.

Florida Rivers On Old Picture Postcards. Ormond Beach, Florida: Camelot Publishing, 2002.

Jacksonville: A Historic Tour In Picture Postcards. Ormond Beach, Florida: Camelot Publishing, 2002

The Ocklawaha River On Old Picture Postcards. Ormond Beach, Florida: Camelot Publishing, 2002.

Volusia County Postcards: Windows to our Past. Ormond Beach, Florida: Camelot Publishing, 2001.

Stowe, Harriet Beecher. *Palmetto Leaves*. Boston, Massachusetts: James R. Osgood and Co., 1873.

Torrey, Bradford. *A Florida Sketch-Book*. Boston, Massachusetts: Houghton, Mifflin and Company, 1894.

Van Doren, Mark. *Travels of William Bartram, Editor*. New York, New York: Dover Publications, Inc., 1955.

Ward, James Robertson. *Old Hickory's Town: An Illustrated History of Jacksonville*. Jacksonville: Florida Publishing Company, 1982.

Watson, Henry B. *Bicentennial Pictorial History of Volusia County*. Daytona Beach, Florida: The News Journal Corporation, 1976.

Werry, Howard. *Florida's Early Pioneers: Struggling with the Wilderness*. Orlando, Florida: Wilmot Publishing Company, 1987.

Winn, Ed. *The Early History of the St. Johns River*. Maitland, Florida: Winn's Books, date unknown.

Wood, Wayne W. *Jacksonville's Architectural Heritage*. Gainesville, Florida: University Press of Florida, 1989.

Index

MORE SCHIFFER TITLES

www.schifferbooks.com

Greetings from Daytona Beach. Donald D. Spencer. The rich past of Daytona Beach is revisited through rare postcard views of one of Floridas most scenic and historic areas. A wonderful selection of over 260 charming scenes display Daytona Beach when visitors went to the ocean in heavy woolen bathing suits and automobiles brought changes that transformed the area. Accompanied by an engaging account of local history and lore, the images document the first half of the twentieth century and illustrate architectural embellishments and unique designs.

Size: 11" x 8 1/2"   259 color photos
ISBN: 978-0-7643-2896-0

Index/Price Guide   128 pp.
soft cover $24.95

Greetings from Tampa. Donald D. Spencer. The Tampa Bay, on Florida's gulf coast, has been inhabited since ancient times by the Indians, Spanish explorers, and English settlers, but it wasn't until Fort Brooke was established in 1824 that true development began. Over 300 postcards show Tampa's history from 1902 to 1950. Long-time and new residents of the city, and visitors will find it fascinating. Approximate dates and values of the postcards make this a wonderful reference.

Size: 11" x 8 1/2"   314 vintage postcards   Price Guide/Index   128 pp.
ISBN: 978-0-7643-2898-5   soft cover $24.95

Greetings from Ormond Beach, Florida. Donald D. Spencer. From early hand-colored cards to photographic views in both color and black and white, this extensive collection of postcards yields a unique glimpse of Ormond Beach, Florida, during the first half of the twentieth century. Over 230 postcards portray the people, street views, hotels, parks, race cars, residences, churches, and gardens of this special place and captions offer little-known history and lore.

Size: 11" x 8 1/2"   238 color photos
ISBN: 978-0-7643-2809-1

Index/Price Guide   128 pp.
soft cover $24.95

Greetings from St. Augustine. Donald D. Spencer. St. Augustine encapsulates nearly 500 years of fascinating history. Established along Floridas northeast coast in 1565, is the oldest city in America. Over 300 vintage hand-tinted postcards from the 1900s through the 1950s take readers on a visual tour. Witness some of the events and places that have made St. Augustine one of the most interesting cities in America.

Size: 11" x 8 1/2"   303 color postcards   Price Guide/Index   128 pp.
ISBN: 978-0-7643-2802-2   soft cover $24.95

Schiffer books may be ordered from your local bookstore, or they may be ordered directly from the publisher by writing to:
Schiffer Publishing, Ltd.
4880 Lower Valley Rd
Atglen PA 19310
(610) 593-1777; Fax (610) 593-2002
E-mail: Info@schifferbooks.com

Please visit our web site catalog at **www.schifferbooks.com** or write for a free catalog. Please include $5.00 for shipping and handling for the first two books and $2.00 for each additional book. Full-price orders over $150 are shipped free in the U.S.

Printed in China

St. Johns River begins in the swamps in southeast Florida, then passes through many lakes, communities, forests, and swamps for 310 miles northward towards the Atlantic Ocean near Jacksonville. It is a resource that has been enjoyed by millions, but few know its full and fascinating story: Like its exploration by both the Spanish and French, how it hosted a thriving Steamboat trade, and has been a popular recreational and tourist site.

Illustrated by nearly 300 vintage postcards, author Donald D. Spencer, who has written several books about Florida's more popular beaches and sites, takes the reader on a virtual tour from St. Johns source to its basin, giving insight into its history, tributaries, cities and attractions along the river.

US $24.99

9 780764 328268   52499

ISBN: 978-0-7643-2826-8